FRANK LUCAS WITH ALIYA S. KING

ORIGINAL GANG$TER

MY LIFE AS NYC'S BIGGEST BADDEST DRUGS BARON

EBURY
PRESS

1 3 5 7 9 10 8 6 4 2

This edition published 2012
First published in 2010 by Ebury Press, an imprint of Ebury Publishing
A Random House Group company
First published in the USA by St. Martin's Press in 2010

The Random House Group Limited Reg. No. 954009

Addresses for companies within the Random House Group can be found at
www.randomhouse.co.uk

A CIP catalogue record for this book is available
from the British Library

The Random House Group Limited supports The Forest Stewardship
Council (FSC®), the leading international forest certification organisation.
Our books carrying the FSC label are printed on FSC® certified paper.
FSC is the only forest certification scheme endorsed by the leading
environmental organisations, including Greenpeace. Our paper
procurement policy can be found at www.randomhouse.co.uk/environment

MIX
Paper from
responsible sources
FSC® C016897

Printed and bound in Great Britain by
CPI Cox & Wyman, Reading RG1 8EX

ISBN 9780091928674

To buy books by your favourite authors and register for offers visit
www.randomhouse.co.uk

I would like to dedicate this book to all the kids who will read it, including Richard Robertson, my four sons and four daughters, and especially my youngest son, Ray. Please learn from my mistakes that I have made throughout my life and do not go the route that I took. Please stay in school, finish high school, and earn the highest-level degree in education that you can. This is the way to go in life.

Sincerely,

Mr. Frank Lucas

ACKNOWLEDGMENTS

I would like to acknowledge the following people. First of all my mother, Mahelee Lucas. Please rest in peace, I love you always. My father, Fred, who is also deceased, please rest in peace. Thank you both dearly.

My partner, Julie Farrait (Lucas), my children, Betty Lucas, Ruby Lucas, Tony Walters, Candace Lucas, Frank Lucas, Francine Lucas-Sinclair, and Ray Lucas. I love each and every one of you in my own special way. Thank you for supporting and being there for me throughout the years.

My brothers, Ezell, Larry, and Leevon Lucas. Also, to my brothers who have passed away, Vernon Lee and John Paul, please rest in peace. I appreciate all your family support and help.

My in-laws, Ernesto and Julia Farrait. Rest in peace and thank you for being there for Francine when her parents could not be.

My brothers-in-law, Ernesti Farrait and Cesar Farrait, thank you for always being there for Julie and me throughout the years.

My grandchildren, thank you for making life so tranquil. I am honored.

Madrina Gachon, who was the "God Mother of All." Thank you for being there, too.

Mr. "Bumpy" Johnson, the one and only boss. Bumpy, thank you for teaching me, but now I look back and I think I would have been better off without the knowledge you gave me. Rest in peace.

The great champion boxer Joe Louis and his wife, Martha Louis. Thank you for everything you did for my family and me. I know you are up there still looking down on me and wishing me the best in life. Rest in peace.

Also, I would like to acknowledge the people at Universal Studios and Imagine Entertainment: Grant Gullickson, Ron Howard, Sarah Bowen, Ridley Scott, Brian Grazer, and Jim Whitaker. Thank you for all your help in making my life appear on the big screen and making *American Gangster* one of the all-time classics.

The one and only Denzel Washington. I love you, Denzel. You played my character to the "T" in the movie *American Gangster*. Thank you for spending time with me to learn and understand the character that you portrayed in the movie. I appreciate it.

I would also like to thank the entire cast who played in the movie *American Gangster*, especially, Armand Assante, Cuba Gooding Jr., Common, Ruby Dee, James Brolin, and T I. You guys all portrayed my lifestyle the way it was back in the 1970s.

Richard M. Roberts, my friend forever. Thank you, Richard, for everything that you have done, did, and still do for me.

Marc Jacobson and Nick Pileggi are also to credit for getting my story and the movie made. Marc, you are an incredible writer. Nick, you are the best "Godfather" anyone could ever have. Thank you both.

Aliya S. King, for writing my life story: you were the best writing partner anyone could hope for—spending over six months with me during the process. All the draft copies and rewrites of the book you spent so much time working on—I really appreciate it. Aliya, thank you so much from the bottom of my heart.

Marc Gerald and Andy Roth at The Agency Group. Thank you so much for putting together all the pieces of my book and speaking engagements. It is a great honor to work with both of you.

My attorneys, Hayes Michel, Irving Tobin, and Howard Wasserman. Without your help this book would not have been completed. Thank you for all your help and support.

Ebury and St. Martin's Press, for the publication of my life story. Thank you so much.

My managers, Michael A. Graziano, Dorsey James, Anita Seabron-Davis, Dr. Lori Melman, Darnell Davis, and Louis G. Schornstein. Thank you for persevering and giving up so much time to help me get this book done. I really appreciate it. Michael, my friend and my primary contact guy, I love you, buddy, thank you so much from the bottom of my heart.

Cates and Ralph White, the best security guys ever. Alamo Al, the best driver of them all. Al, thank you for driving me to all my events. Thank you to Timothy Drake Green and his partner Alexis Culcleasure.

The one and only Pam Frazier. You are the best, and thank you for all your help.

My great-great-goddaughter, Gianna Rose. You are such a special person to me. I know your parents, Michael and Lori, are truly blessed to have you.

Derrick "Sosa" Dicker, for putting together the "Frank Lucas Clothing" line. I truly appreciate your hard work and effort and for making the line become a reality. I look forward to everyone wearing FL—the Frank Lucas clothing in the near future.

Lastly, Bodine, Cookie, and Ricky. Thank you for your help and support.

1

It's been more than seventy years. But I can see the whole thing as clear as a bell. I wasn't but six years old and I was wearing those redfooted pajamas with the flap on the butt. Something woke me up with a start. It was early morning, summer of 1936.

I looked toward the front door of the one-room shack I shared with my parents in rural North Carolina. My favorite cousin, Obadiah Biden, had been staying with us. We usually slept together on a straw pallet on the floor. But when I woke up, Obadiah wasn't there.

There was a group of loud, angry men yelling outside our house and Obadiah was on his way to the front door to see what was going on.

My father was away for a few days and we were alone with my mother. I remember getting out of bed, listening in fear to the sounds of men yelling out for my cousin to come to the door. In front of me was a chair with a shirt hanging on it. I put it on over my pajamas to cover myself up. I even remember that the shirt was much too big for me and hung down to my knees. I think it was either my father's shirt or Obadiah's.

"Obadiah, what's going on?" I asked, rubbing my eyes and trying to sit up.

"Stay here, Frank," my cousin told me.

"Come out here, nigger! NOW!" I heard a man scream. The harsh sound of the man's voice made me jump. My blood went cold and I watched my cousin's fearful face as he stood by the door.

"If you don't come out here right now, we're coming in to get you!" another of the men yelled out.

Obadiah opened the front door and was snatched up by the three men who had come to our home looking for him. All of them were white and beefy—perfect examples of what you would call rednecks.

Our small shack had a wide wraparound porch. So, as soon as Obadiah was snatched out the front door, I slipped around to the side of the house to peek out and see what was going on.

I still wish I hadn't done that.

I craned my neck to look around to the front of the house to try and make out what was going on. It was almost too much for my six-year-old mind to comprehend.

Those three white men, thick and rugged, converged on my cousin Obadiah, tussling and struggling with him while yelling and cursing.

"You ought to know better than to be staring at no girl around here, nigger," said one of them, a tall man with small, beady eyes.

He took a long piece of rope and twisted it around my cousin's wrist. He then took the slack of the rope and tied a knot around Obadiah's other wrist, as the other men held him.

The men pulled the ropes tight, so that Obadiah was forced to stand with his hands spread out. And then I watched, in horror, as the man stepped close to my cousin's face.

He said, "You eyeballing a white girl? Is that what you want, nigga? You want a white girl?" And then he slammed Obadiah in the mouth with the butt of his gun. Obadiah had broken teeth and blood spewing out of his mouth, and a feeling of rage and fear hit my gut hard.

That man then brought his double-barreled shotgun up and shoved the gun as far down my cousin's throat as he could while his partners held Obadiah tight.

"Look here, nigga. This is what happens when you look at white girls you ain't got no business looking at."

And then he positioned his fingers on both triggers. And pulled them both at the same time.

My cousin Obadiah was my best friend. He was like a brother to me. He would take me to the store occasionally to buy me penny candy, if he had a penny. He took me out to the woods and taught me everything from how to use a slingshot to how to make a ball out of twine. He took me fishing and sometimes he'd even let me shoot off his rifle in the woods.

Obadiah Biden was my hero. And that night, I watched my favorite cousin, his head completely blown apart by the gunshot blast, fall into a crumpled heap in the dirt in front of our home. Let me explain to you what I saw. You need to know exactly what I'm talking about. From the front—my dead cousin Obadiah looked the same. But in the back, there was no back. You could fit a melon in the hole they blasted in the back of his head.

He was thirteen years old.

I saw something that morning that no child should ever see. I was a witness to something so bloody, brutal, and vicious that I have never been the same.

I couldn't get the image of Obadiah's crumpled, bloody corpse out of my mind. And so I ran, as far and as fast as my little tiny legs could take me. I was still wearing my pajamas. But I was just so scared that I didn't know what else to do. I ran out into the woods and kept moving until the woods were so thick with brush that I couldn't go any farther.

I sat down on the ground, hugging my knees to my chest, rocking back and forth, and crying my eyes out. I couldn't imagine what Obadiah could have done to make those men do that to him. My cousin was a good, decent kid. Barely a teenager. And they had killed him in cold blood in front of me and my mother. I cried harder and harder, trying to get the picture out of my mind. After a while, I must have fallen asleep out there. 'Cause the next thing I remember was hearing a man's voice yelling out my name.

"Frank! Frank Lucas, are you out here!"

I woke up frightened. I thought it could have been those white men who'd killed my cousin. As far as I knew, they could be coming back to kill me. So I didn't answer.

"Frank? Did you hear me calling you, boy?"

I looked up to see my father, sweaty and out of breath, standing right next to me. I jumped up and ran to him. I hadn't even known he'd returned from his trip, and I was very relieved to see him.

"Why would you run away like that? Your mother's been worried sick, looking for you!"

"I was scared. You saw what they did to Cousin Obadiah?"

My dad picked me up and started walking back through the woods to our shack.

"Yes, Frank. I saw it all."

We went back to the house and I saw my parents speaking to each other in low voices. Their faces were full of worry.

My mother was a handsome woman, small in stature with cocoa-brown skin. Even though she wasn't a tall woman, there was something about her that just exuded power and confidence. A look from my mother could freeze a grown person in his tracks. My father wasn't a tall man, either. But again, he wasn't someone you wanted to mess with. He had a broad body with wide shoulders and looked liked he could break a person in two with his bare hands. He wasn't a friendly man. He was more focused on taking care of his family in a tough time. Can't say I saw either of my parents smile too much. And they weren't particularly affectionate toward me and my younger siblings or to each other.

But it was a different time period. Parents weren't touchy-feely with their kids. You were just lucky to keep them alive. Danger lurked around every corner in my parents' day. You never knew if you would have enough food to eat. Or if something like what happened to Obadiah was on the horizon.

Three days after Obadiah's murder, my father hitched up a mule and wagon and we rode a few miles out to Rockford Church, where our pastor, Peter Hood, preached the funeral for my cousin. It was the saddest thing you'd ever want to see. I could not stop crying throughout the ceremony. Not just because Obadiah was dead, but the way he died—so violently and senselessly. I couldn't get that scene out of my head, no matter how hard I tried. And I wasn't just sad—I was enraged.

What happened to my family was not unusual. In those days, it happened way more than it ever should have. Something changed within me. I often wonder what kind of man I would have turned out to be if my cousin Obadiah had not been killed right in front of me. Maybe I would have stayed in La Grange. Maybe I would have become a sharecropper like my parents, farming tobacco and living off the land. I have no idea. But I do know that Obadiah's death had a profound effect on my development. After his funeral, I knew I'd never be the same.

My family was helpless. The men who had killed my cousin were members of the Ku Klux Klan. And they ruled over black people in the South with an iron fist. But my father was not going to let Obadiah die in vain. He went into town a few days later to talk to the sheriff about what had happened to his nephew and demand that the Klansmen be arrested. That discussion ended when the sheriff put my daddy out of his office. He said something like, "Nigga, get your ass outta here before I lock you up."

My daddy went home and he was pissed off. Told everyone who would listen how he was gonna get the sheriff for disrespecting him like that. "I'ma kill 'im," he kept saying over and over.

Word got back to the sheriff that my daddy was talking about getting back at him. And so a day or two after my daddy talked to him, here comes the sheriff.

I was there, along with my parents. I stood right there and watched as that white man came into our house and asked my dad if it was true that he was talking about getting back at them.

"You ain't doing nothing to nobody," the sheriff said to my father, who had a stony, blank look on his face. "You ain't doing a goddamn thing."

I'm not exactly sure what happened next. Maybe the sheriff went to slap Daddy or something like that. All I know is that before I could blink twice, those two were fighting all over the house, knocking over things and wrestling all over the bed my parents shared. I stayed close to my mother, frightened.

The sheriff ran out of the house to his car to get his shotgun. But before he could even turn back around, my father had got his own shotgun, pointed it at the man, and squeezed off with both barrels. I will never forget that sheriff. He wasn't fat, but he had a big ass and was wearing white pants. And as soon as my daddy shot him, we saw a bright spot of red spreading across the back of those white pants.

That sheriff hopped into the car and drove away real fast.

Now here we are. My father shot the sheriff. He was not going to be able to just sit there to wait for whomever they sent to arrest him. They wouldn't just lock him up. They'd kill him. My father took off, planning to hide in the woods for as long as he needed to.

In the span of one week, my whole family structure had fallen apart. First, my cousin had been killed. Then my dad had to leave. My mom, a hardworking woman who was as strong as any man I knew, was left alone as my dad went into hiding. And I, at six years old, was now the man of the house.

And my family was going to have to eat. Even though my mother never came right out and told me she would need help to feed the family, I knew I would have to do something.

Someone once said that hunger makes a thief of any man. And I believe that's true. My life of crime began at age six. I became a thief so that my family could eat—plain and simple. And I continued my life on the wrong side of the law until I became one of the biggest, most notorious criminals that the United States can lay claim to.

A few days after my daddy went into hiding, he returned.

"Daddy!" I yelled out, when I saw him at the front door.

"Shhhh," my mother whispered, covering my mouth with her hand. "You trying to get your daddy killed? No one can know he's here."

My dad crept into the house, hugged my mother and me and my baby brothers. He had a dead squirrel and a few rabbits he'd killed out in the woods and he gave them to my mother so she could make stew out of them.

"Are you okay out there?" my mother asked my father.

"No," he said. "But I will be."

"When are you going to be able to come home for good?"

"I don't know. When the sheriff stops looking for me, I suppose."

"That might never happen," my mother said, her eyes filling with tears.

"We're gonna be fine," my father said.

After a tear-filled dinner of rabbit stew and vegetables, my father had to take to the woods once again. I cried, knowing I might not see him for another month or possibly longer. He was going to have to stay hidden for as long as possible, until the heat was off.

During my father's absences, I noticed that my mother, as proud as she was, was having a hard time keeping enough food in the house. She had to chop wood for the fires to keep us warm, try to hunt animals for meat, tend to the gardens, and she had to do all the farm work my father normally did. All this and she had to attend to me and all my siblings. Even though I was only six, I was the oldest boy and I knew I had to help.

I began stealing chickens and other livestock from nearby farms to feed my family. I wasn't a natural thief. I was a very good kid—before Obadiah was killed. But after that happened, I was just dead inside. Obadiah was gone. My father was hiding out from the sheriff. I was in survivor mode. My mom needed my help and I was going to do anything in my power to assist her. We lived several miles from the closest farm. I would walk out for miles and miles, until I got to a farm that wasn't well tended. I'd run into the chicken coop and steal chickens and eggs. The next time, I might try to get a goat. Once, I even stole a whole pig and brought it back to my mom.

My mother never asked where I'd gotten the livestock. And I never told her. We both understood what was going on. We had to eat, plain and simple, and she needed my help, even though I was little more than a baby myself.

By the age of nine, I'd moved on to robbing the johns waiting outside Ava Blackman's piccolo joint and whorehouse, a few miles from my family's shack outside La Grange, North Carolina. They'd come out drunk as a skunk and careless. I'd hit them in the head with a brick or a bat, steal their money, and run. It was almost too easy. The first time, I got ten dollars. Might not seem like much today. But back then, it was enough to feed my family for months.

I was a reckless and vicious thief, motivated not by greed but solely by my need to survive.

I will make no excuses for the life I began to lead. But I knew early on that I wasn't going to accept the life my parents had to forge for us. There was just no way. I can't tell you exactly why I turned out the way I did, but I know I've never recovered from seeing what the Klan did to my cousin. They may not have created me, but they damn sure contributed to the man I was to become.

By the time I was a teenager, I'd lived enough for two people. I became too much for my neck of the woods. The last straw was when I broke in to the general store in town and stole four hundred dollars. Four hundred dollars back then felt like all the money in the world. It really felt like a million dollars would to me now. It was a serious crime and I couldn't wait around for them to figure out it was me who did it. I had to leave town.

I went on to Wilson, North Carolina, and stayed with an aunt there while I tried to think of my next step. I'd heard people talking about how Kentucky was called the Bluegrass State and for some reason I kept thinking about that. I wondered if it was true and just what "blue grass" would look like. With the money I had from the general-store robbery, I sent my momma two hundred dollars and got myself a bus ticket to Kentucky.

Now, you have to remember, I was barely thirteen years old at this point. And I was already on my own, trying to find my way as best I could, and usually depending on my skills as a thief to survive.

On the bus to Kentucky, we stopped in Knoxville, Tennessee. There was a layover for an hour. So I got out and started walking around. About three blocks from the bus station, I found a group of men playing a craps game against the wall of an abandoned factory. I perked up. This would be a way for me to get some money. Back in North Carolina, I had learned how to play craps from hanging around the whorehouse, waiting to rob the drunken customers.

Craps is a game of chance; you're either hot or you're cold. For some reason, I was often hot with a pair of dice in my hand.

At first, I just observed, keeping an eye on how much money they had.

"You trying to get in this game or what?" one guy said. He looked like he was a few years older than me. Taller than me but not much.

"What they rolling for?" I asked.

"Dollar . . ."

A dollar was a lot of money in 1943. So I knew these kids had probably come up on some money the same way I had—robbing someone or something. Didn't matter to me: I had more than a few dollars to bet.

I held my hands out and he dropped the dice in my hand. I shook them in my hand until they felt right.

The four young men standing around me placed their bets, all of them mumbling, "Pass," or "Don't pass," eyeing me warily as they spoke.

Now that my bet had been covered by the young men, I could roll the dice. I held my hand up near my shoulder, shook the dice vigorously a few times, and tossed the dice against the building.

I quickly found myself on the right side of Lady Luck. The dollar bills piled up at my feet as I continued to throw the dice, winning turn after turn.

"Shit," one guy whispered after he lost another dollar. He rolled his eyes and dug his hands into his pockets to get another dollar out.

As the game intensified, we all began to crouch lower to the ground, whispering and trash talking.

"Nigga, yo' luck 'bout to run out," said the tall guy.

"You wish," I said with a smile, shaking my fist and throwing the dice with an elaborate flourish.

I won again and the tall guy sucked his teeth. "This is some bullshit," he said.

Finally, I rolled a seven and my turn was up. I leaned down to pick up my money.

"Ai-ight, fellas, I got a bus to catch," I said, straightening up and then turning around.

"Nigga, you ain't going nowhere with my fucking money," said the tall guy.

Before he could say another word, I jumped him and started punching him as hard as I could in the face. There was no need to talk. I knew he was pissed that I'd beaten him so bad, so it made sense to just go ahead and get a head start.

But of course, I was there alone. And the rest of the guys were on his side. One of them jumped on my back and we were all fighting, rolling around on the ground. I tried to stand up, threw one guy off my back, then turned to punch him. But just when I pulled my hand back, the whole world went black. I guess somebody hit me in the head with something. I don't know. I woke up facedown in a creek with my eyes sealed shut with blood.

When I finally came to, I dragged myself out of the creek. I was dirty, hungry, and cold. And all my money was gone. My bus to Kentucky had gone on without me and now I was broke and without a place to say.

I went to the general store in town and the door was open. I stole a johnnycake, a piece of cheese, and a Pepsi. I sat there, wincing every time I took a bite because my jaw hurt so bad. I just tried to focus on taking a deep breath and getting my strength up so I could figure out how I was going to get out of town.

"Put your hands right where I can see 'em," I heard someone say. I froze. And I heard the clop of hard shoes walking toward me. The cops. Damn.

"Officer, I was attacked a few hours ago and I—"

"Nigger, close your mouth until I tell you to speak."

I heard the *click* of the safety being taken off the officer's weapon.

"Stand up," he said.

I exhaled. And then I stood up, keeping my hands above my head.

"Breaking and entering the general store. Larceny. And you look like the young man I'm hearing got off the bus from Kentucky and started gambling and robbing folks."

"I ain't rob nobody."

"I said shut your mouth," he said, getting real close to my face and talking through clenched teeth.

He led me down the street to the town jail, which was just a few doors down from the general store. I spent the night in jail, and the next morning I was taken before a judge.

I was still sick as a dog and felt half dead when I went to see the judge. He was talking so fast that I didn't know what he was saying. I had no attorney. No one asked me if I was guilty or innocent. I couldn't tell you what I was officially charged with or how long I was being sentenced. I came in there, listened to the judge mumble something. And then five minutes later, he said, "Take him on down to John's gang." He banged his gavel and that was that. Someone led me away from the courthouse in handcuffs.

Next thing I remember, I was being taken to the side of a dirt road. I saw a white man sitting high up on a horse. The man on the horse had a fat pink face and he was furiously chewing tobacco and spitting it out, letting the drool catch on his chin.

"He's all yours," said the man who had brought me.

The man on the horse laughed out loud. "Hell, I'm gon' do with him?"

The other man shrugged. "Judge sent him. Do what you want."

I looked around and saw at least two dozen black men, chained together at their feet. They were digging a ditch along the side of the road. A few of them looked up at me and then quickly put their heads right back down and focused on their shovels and the dirt at their feet.

The man who had brought me over from the courthouse disappeared. And someone else came over and attached a leg shackle to my ankle and then connected me to the rest of the gang.

"Here," the man said, putting a shovel in my hand. "Dig."

The sun was so hot overhead that I could see wavy lines in the sky. Had to be ninety degrees. At least. Beads of sweat were pouring down everyone's head, even the white men on horseback, who weren't doing any work.

An elderly black man was the only person not shackled. He was carrying a bucket of water and a tin cup and holding it out for the prisoners to get an occasional sip. After an hour, he came over to me and offered me water.

"What's your name, boy?" he whispered.

"Frank Lucas," I said, darting my eyes over at the white man on horseback.

"Frank, you gotta get outta here," he said. "You gonna be here for an awfully long time if you don't."

"Jimmy Reed, who you talking to over there, boy?"

Jimmy quickly rushed down to the next man on line.

"Ain't talking to nobody, Captain Charlie, nobody at *all.*"

"I got my eye on you, Jimmy Reed. Nigger, you better not blink too fast or I will shoot you and bury you right here in this ditch."

I actually had no idea how much time that judge gave me. So Jimmy Reed was probably right. If I didn't escape, I'd be there forever. But I wasn't sure what I was going to do about it, and I told him so later on that night, when we were all at the mess hall of the small prison.

"I don't know how you gon' do it. But I'm gon' help you," Jimmy Reed said.

"Why?" I asked. "Why you helping me?"

"What you mean why? Boy, you ain't but thirteen. You can't be here. It's not right. You gotta go."

I looked around at the other men on the chain gang. I hadn't spoken to any of them. And they didn't look like they had two words for me, either.

"Don't worry about them," Jimmy Reed said. "Worry about you. And pay attention tomorrow."

The chain gang was watched over by a group of white men on horseback. We called them all Captain Charlie. Each of us had a thick chain and a lock on our ankles. Most of the work was ditch digging. For the next few days, I just dug my ditch and watched. Occasionally, Jimmy Reed would nudge me and I'd look up and see the white man on the horse take a sip from a flask and then shudder.

After a few days, Jimmy Reed cleared his throat one morning and spoke directly to the mounted officer.

"Thinking Frank can just help me get the water for us," he said.

"Dat boy can dig like the rest of them. You're the only nigga not worth working."

"Just thinking he looks peaked," said Jimmy Reed. "Be a pain to deal with a dead body. Alls I'm saying . . ."

The guard looked at me and I made sure to look as pathetic as possible. I even coughed.

The guard took a swig from his flask and shuddered. Then he gestured to one of the men who worked for him and said, "G'wan and take his irons off."

Someone came over and released me from the rest of the chain gang and I immediately started rubbing my ankle, where it was sore from the chains.

"You stand right here next to me," said Captain Charlie. "You move and I will kill you."

I had to stand right near the men on horseback and I

could never leave their sight. If I had to use the bathroom, they gave me a few feet of twine to hold on to. They would hold the beginning of the rope, and if I had to go a bit out of the way to use the bathroom in the woods, they could make sure I was still nearby.

One day, Jimmy Reed gave me some extra twine and I hid it inside my pants. He gave me a look and I knew what it meant. Time to go. The next time I needed to use the bathroom, I handed the beginning of the rope to the man I called Captain Charlie.

"I gotta go take one, Captain Charlie," I said.

"Stay where I can hear you. You know what to do," he said.

Every few seconds he expected to hear me say, "Shaking the bush, Captain Charlie, shaking the bush!" At the same time, I was supposed to yank at the twine we both held to let him know that I was still holding on to it. With this method, he could make sure I was nearby in two ways—from the sound of my voice and the feel of me pulling on the twine—even if he couldn't see me.

He didn't bank on me having more twine than I usually had. So I kept moving through the woods every ten seconds yelling out, "Shaking the bush, Captain Charlie" and continuing to yank on the rope.

I came to a fence and realized it was time to make a break for it. At the same time, Captain Charlie realized that my voice was coming from just a bit too far away. I heard the sound of Captain Charlie galloping toward me just as I got ready to break free.

I leaped over the fence, Captain Charlie at my heels. If his horse had not changed his mind about jumping that fence at the last minute, I wouldn't be here to tell the tale. But as it stands, Captain Charlie got thrown over that fence like something out of a movie. That didn't stop him from shooting at me though.

I heard the bullets whiz by my ear. Heard 'em twice, as a matter of fact. I heard the bullets pass me. And then I heard myself pass those bullets!

I continued running on the side of a dirt road until I came across a black family on their way to California with all their possessions. I hitched a ride with them and they told me they would take me out as far as they could.

They dropped me off in Lexington on their way to the West Coast. I was thirteen years old, alone, and flat broke. And I was in a state I'd never been to before. It was late fall. It was just starting to get cold, and the first night, I slept under a house. All the houses out there were set off the ground and there was usually enough crawl space to sleep and be warm.

After three or four nights of sleeping under one house, the young man who lived there caught me and told his mother that I was out there.

I had been leaving during the day to find food—eating whatever I could. Even stuff out of the garbage when I had to. And then at night, I was going back under their house.

"How long you been hiding out under my house, young man?" the woman asked.

"Few days, ma'am. Ain't mean no harm. Just ain't got nowhere to stay."

"Well, good Lord, ya ask someone for help. Don't just sleep under a house. Ain't safe. And way too cold for you, besides. You look liked death warmed over. Sit."

I sat at her round kitchen table. Her home was nicer than

any I'd ever been to. It was a real house, not a shack on the bare dirt floor like we had in North Carolina.

Looking back, the house wasn't anything special. No indoor plumbing or anything fancy like that. But she had an icebox stocked with food in her large kitchen. And the smells of fresh-baked bread, ham hocks, and collard greens mingled together with the lemony smell of whatever she used to scrub her floors. It felt like a home. A warm, cozy home. It was something I knew nothing about.

Family's name was Jones. A single mother and a few kids, including the son who had caught me sleeping there. Mrs. Jones took me in, fed me, and gave me some decent clothes to wear.

"We ain't got much," she said, handing over a pair of clean pants and a clean shirt. "But I ain't gon' let you go hungry."

" 'Preciate it," I said.

"House'll be empty soon anyway," she said, gesturing toward her son, whose head was buried in a book.

"Is that so?" I asked.

"All my kids are in college," said Mrs. Jones. She beamed. "On their way back for the new semester in a few days."

I nodded. The concept of college was stranger than indoor plumbing and a full icebox to me.

"So you can earn your keep 'round here," she said. "Be nice if you could get the fire started each morning. I like it warm in here by six."

"Yes, ma'am. Not a problem," I said, shoveling the food she set before me into my mouth.

"Use a fork, chil'," she said, smiling. "Food ain't going nowhere and there's more where that came from."

One morning, about three months after I arrived, I woke up and it was as cold as a black whore's heart. The kids were all away at school and it was usually just us in the house in the morning. Mrs. Jones was a bootlegger and she'd start mixing her batches early in the morning while I would go out and run the streets, gambling, fighting, and whatever else. My favorite thing to do was go to the pool hall near the bus station. I was learning a mean game of pool from a couple of older guys who hung out there all day. I took quickly to the game and they even started having me play for money against other men.

That morning, before leaving for the pool hall, I went into the main room to get the fire started as usual. From the area where the fireplace was located, I could see where Mrs. Jones slept. Usually she was covered up in the blankets, sleeping heavily until the small house was warm.

But this time, she was already awake.

"Mornin'," I said, using the poker to stoke the embers.

Mrs. Jones stretched her legs and I saw her brown foot, ankle, leg, and then thigh creep into view. I turned around quickly and focused back on the fire.

Now remember, I am barely thirteen years old. And this woman was old enough to be my grandmother. I'd messed around with young girls my age in North Carolina here and there, but nothing serious. Mrs. Jones was a whole different story. She was a grown woman.

I could hear Mrs. Jones sit up in bed.

"Frank, what you working with over there?"

" 'Scuse me?"

"Come here, Frank."

I walked over to the side of her bed, keeping my head down.

"Yes, ma'am."

"Look at me."

I looked up. Mrs. Jones might have been an older woman, but she sure was pretty. Cocoa-brown skin. Full lips. Great head of hair.

She pulled the covers back and I like to had a heart attack.

"They got all this where you come from in North Carolina?"

"Reckon they do," I said, running a hand over my face.

"You know what to do with it?"

"Reckon I do," I said.

"Well, let's go."

After a few months of our new arrangement, it was time for me to move on. I've never been one to live off someone. It just didn't feel right. I needed to make my own way. I don't think Mrs. Jones had any idea how young I was. By the time I was thirteen, I was as tall as I am right now. And I was often mistaken for someone much older. Only old Jimmy Reed was able to see that I was just a kid. Everyone else treated me as if I were at least five or ten years older.

After four or five months, me and Mrs. Jones went our separate ways. I ended up working in a nearby pipe factory. Can't remember how I came to start working there. Maybe Mrs. Jones put in a good word for me. But somehow, I managed to get a job on the assembly line, double-checking the various parts of the pipes before they got boxed up and shipped out.

One morning, I was standing on the assembly line when Kennedy, the owner of the warehouse, walked through, talking to some other people and pointing things out in the factory. He had a young girl with him. She was taking notes while everyone else was talking.

"You better stop looking at that girl," said one of my co-workers.

"Tell her to stop looking at *me*," I said.

"That's Kennedy's daughter," my co-worker said. "Name's Lucy. And she'll get you in a heap of trouble, so stay away from her."

That white girl was fine. Thick girl. Had a little something in all the right places. Legs went on and on for days. Bright red hair, green eyes, and a face full of freckles. And there was something mysterious behind her smile. She looked like the type who liked to get in trouble. And I was the type to help her out.

"Frank! Psst. Frank!"

I was on my lunch break, about two weeks after I had started working at Kennedy's factory. Lucy had given me the eye more than once. But I would just look the other way. Finally, she'd had enough of my silent treatment. She found a reason to come near my side of the break room and pretended to talk to me about something work related.

"I'm going to need to see you in my office," she said.

"I didn't know you had an office," I said, keeping my eyes on my lunch.

"Right 'round by the side exit. Five minutes," she said, before walking away.

Now, I could have ignored her. I knew what she wanted and the feelings were mutual. But I knew firsthand what happened to black men who were even accused of just looking at a white girl. Especially the boss's daughter. But this was when I first discovered something important about my personality: I didn't give a good goddamn about nothing.

I know for a fact that my attitude had everything to do with what I saw happen to my cousin Obadiah. That erased any filter I had. I would never go with the status quo. I'd do what I wanted and dare someone to make me pay the price.

Five minutes later, I was sneaking away from the assembly line and looking for Lucy. The office she'd mentioned was anything but. It was just a small storage area I'd never noticed. Nothing but broken equipment in a dark, dank room.

"Anybody in here?" I asked.

"Back here, Frank. Hurry!"

I took a few more steps forward and it got so dark I could barely see two feet in front of me. I could hear Lucy's voice but I couldn't see her at all.

"What in the hell—"

I felt a hand grab my shirt and pull me down. Lucy had some kind of pallet down on the floor. We both fell down on top of it and I realized she was completely naked. I almost passed out in sheer shock. And after I ran my hands over her body, I almost passed out again, for other reasons.

We weren't in that storage area very long, but it felt like a lifetime to me. And that became my lunchtime ritual. Lucy wasn't in the factory every day. But when she was, I was sure to hear a "psst, Frank" in the break room. And I knew what was going to go down.

Week after week, month after month, the routine was the same. I'd be working and she would pop up, give me the eye, and I'd meet her at the back of the warehouse.

One afternoon, disaster struck. A white guy who worked near me on the assembly line had been giving me funny looks for a week. I should have known he was on to us. But of course, I didn't care. He followed me while I was following Lucy. Just as soon as me and Lucy got into it, I heard the rustling of furniture being moved and then the spotlight of a flashlight on me and Lucy.

"When Kennedy finds out about this, you a dead nigger," the man said.

Lucy grabbed a shirt to cover herself and pointed a finger at the man. "You son of a bitch! You tell my daddy and I'll tell him you tried to rape me."

They went back and forth while I got dressed and got the hell out of there. Whether or not Kennedy was going to find out, I knew that was the end of that job. It was time to hit the road—again. The factory still owed me fifty dollars in salary. And I wasn't about to go up to Kennedy and get it from him. Instead, I snuck back into the factory that night, stole a couple hundred dollars, and left for the bus station.

I knew I had to leave the South for good. I decided to make my way to a place I'd only heard about. A place where hundreds of thousands of black folks lived in their own community and the one place where I thought I might actually have a chance to make some real money.

In the summer of 1944, I got off a Greyhound bus at Fiftieth Street and Eighth Avenue in New York City. I had had cardboard lining my shoes. I hopped on a city bus and told the driver where I wanted to go.

When I got off, I looked around, confused. There was nothing but white people, bustling here and there, going into different office buildings. I walked over to a police officer nearby. Didn't really want to talk to a cop, but the regular white folks actually looked more intimidating.

"I'm trying to get to where all the colored people are," I said.

"You see that sign right there?" he asked.

I looked up. The street sign said Fourteenth Street. But that didn't mean anything to me.

"You are on Fourteenth Street. You need to get to One Hundred Fourteenth Street!"

"I don't have any more money," I told the police officer.

The cop gave me a strange look and then shook his head. He took me to the corner and flagged down a bus.

"Take this boy up to One Hundred Fourteenth Street," he told the bus driver. "He just got up here. Ran out of money."

At the time, I remember wondering how he knew I had just come to town. And then I was trying to figure out why the bus driver gave me such a funny look. And then, when I got on the bus, every passenger on that bus moved straight to the back. Wasn't till years later, when I looked back, that I realized that I had been a mess. Smelled to high heaven. Hadn't had a decent shower in weeks. No haircut in months. Had been wearing the same clothes for I don't know how long. I stunk that bus up but good! That driver burned rubber getting up to Harlem. And when he got to 114th Street, he rushed me off that bus real quick.

"Right here! Go. Get off! This is Harlem."

I stood on 114th Street and 8th Avenue and looked to my right and to my left. There was nothing but black people as far as I could see. And there were all kinds of black folks: men and women of all ages and sizes, some who looked dirt poor (but not as poor as me) and some who looked straight-up rich.

I threw out my hands and screamed out as loud as I could, Hello, Harlem USA! I was ready for New York City, but even now, I'm not sure she was ready for me.

2

Harlem was a very different place back in 1944. The neighborhood began as farmland in the 1800s. Then the Irish came, then the Italians, and then the Jews. Finally, beginning in 1904, black folks started pouring uptown.

A few years before I came up from the South, the Harlem River Houses had opened. It was the first federally funded housing project, and when it opened, eleven thousand black folks applied to get in, and there were only about five hundred apartments available. The legendary Apollo Theater had opened up in 1934, ten years before I arrived. And Harlem, when I got there, was almost 100 percent black.

I'd left home a year and a half before. And I'd crammed a whole lifetime into that time. Got locked up, escaped from the chain gang, lived with Mrs. Jones, messed with Lucy Kennedy. And now here I was, just fourteen years old. And I was in New York City, flat broke, with no prospects for money. By day, I wandered around the city, taking in the sights and sounds. It was loud, hot, and sweaty. And I had never seen so many black people in one place in my life. This wasn't rural La Grange, North Carolina. These were black folks who were doing things, going places. They walked with purpose and direction, yelling out to one another in greeting. Talking fast and moving faster. My eyes weren't big enough to take it all in.

I had to get my basic needs met: food and shelter. I saw a diner and decided to go inside and figure out how to get something to eat. I scoped out the situation: a machine at the front counter spat out a ticket, and at each stand you got food and then someone punched your ticket. Then you went to the next station, got more food, and someone punched your ticket again. After your tray was full, you went to a register with a turnstile. You showed your ticket to the cashier, paid your money, and pushed through the turnstile.

I smiled.

I could get my food first and then worry about paying for it. Perfect.

I took a ticket, got some plates, and started filling up. With enough food in several containers to last me a few days, I rushed right past the register, hopped the turnstile, and was out of that cafeteria within seconds. I ran for a few blocks, weaving in and out of the people walking down the street, who had to leap to avoid colliding with me. Finally, I looked back to see if anyone was chasing me. I was safe.

That very moment, I knew I would never go hungry in

New York City. There was just too much of everything. And I was strong enough and brave enough to do whatever I had to do in order to survive.

I ate some of my food in the doorway of a huge apartment building at the corner of 116th Street and 8th Avenue while watching a rowdy craps game taking place. Now it was time to think about shelter. As I ate and watched the older men cursing one another out, I noticed some workmen delivering coal into a side door of the building. In those days, buildings still used coal for heating, not oil or gas. And I knew there had to be some kind of coal room where they stored the coal near the furnace. I slipped into the building and made my way to the basement.

Sure enough, there were a few bums sleeping on their coats on the floor of the coal room. I'd now found a temporary home. That night, I slept on the floor of a coal room in an apartment building at what felt like the center of the universe to me. I had a full belly and a roof over my head. And I planned never to have anything less. I was a long way from home. But now, Harlem was my home.

"Hey, baby, what you know good this morning?"

"I know I need to hit this number, that's all I know!"

"I hear you. What you playing today?"

"Give me a dollar on three ten, that's my momma's birthday."

I stood on the corner of 125th Street and 8th Avenue, quietly observing. As I watched, dozens of people handed over coins and folded bills to a flashy man wearing a suit and tie. He would keep his eyes darting up and down the street and then dip into the store occasionally and come back out, counting his money right there on the street.

I saw my next meal ticket. Any fool dumb enough to count his money on the street, in plain view of a hungry homeless kid with nothing to lose, deserved to get robbed. I didn't act right away, though. First day or two, I just observed. I figured out that there was some kind of unofficial lottery system that he collected money for. I'd never seen anything like it down South. But all I needed to know was that he had cash and he didn't hide it. And I noticed that he was always gone by lunchtime. I assumed that he handed in the money by then. I'd have to get him in the morning.

Just a few days after I'd arrived, I was still stealing food from diners and sleeping in the coal room. And then I committed my first major crime in New York City. Had to be about ten in the morning. Harlem was wide awake and moving. The numbers man was jive talking in his usual spot. I came up slow behind him, right while he was counting his money. While he was licking his thumb, preparing to use it to separate his bills, I reached out, snatched the bills out of his hand, and ran.

"Nigga, get back here with my money!" I heard the man scream out. The clopping sounds of his fancy shoes on the pavement followed me as I wove in and out of the street traffic, running as fast as my cardboard-lined shoes would let me.

I ran to the building I'd been squatting in and then dipped into the side door and went back down to the coal room to count my money.

One hundred dollars. In just ten minutes, I'd made more money than I'd ever made working at the pipe factory. More money than my parents ever made in a whole year of share-cropping.

Robbing that numbers runner was the equivalent of a job interview for me. I had my first gig: a thief.

"Oh shit! Boy, get back here!"

"Fuck! That motherfucker stole my money!"

"Goddammit, somebody call the police, we just got robbed! There he is, right there! He ran that way!"

Over the next few months in Harlem, I got more and more used to hearing sentences like that. I knocked number runners over the head with whatever I could and stole their money; I dashed into corner stores as shopkeepers were just about to buy goods from deliverymen and robbed them. By the time I had enough money to get myself a gun, I was officially a menace to society.

I was an animal, hell-bent on my own survival. Looking back, I don't see how I wasn't killed during my first few months in Harlem. I didn't think about anyone's feelings or well-being. All I cared about was where I was getting my next meal. Within two or three weeks, I had enough money to rent a room at a boardinghouse on 118th Street and 7th Avenue, just a block away from my first home in that coal room with the other homeless bums.

There was an older woman who owned the boarding-house. And I'd only been there for a few weeks when she gave me a certain look that reminded me of that bootlegger Mrs. Jones back in Kentucky. Sure enough, even though the woman who owned the boardinghouse was old enough to be my mother, we started messing around. After a while, I was living rent free in the boardinghouse and she was pro-viding me with all my meals and more.

I never even thought about getting a regular job. That just wasn't me. From the moment I saw my cousin's head blown away in front of me by the Klan, I had no faith in doing things the "right" way. The Klan made up their own rules. And black folks in the South had to live by them. If you broke one of their rules, (or if they just *thought* you did), you ended up like my cousin Obadiah, murdered in cold blood in front of your family. I watched my parents break their backs for next to nothing because they tried to play by the unfair rules of the sharecropping system. Just seemed like trying to do things the so-called right way got you nowhere.

I was going to make up my own rules as I went along.

There were two Harlems back then. There were the high-society folks, the people who lived in the fancy brownstones overlooking Central Park or up on Mount Morris. The good folks with money lived there or over on 138th and 139th between 7th and 8th Avenues.

These folks were nurses and doctors, teachers and college professors who had graduated from black colleges and made a good and decent living. I didn't notice these people. I knew they were there, but it was like they were in black-and-white. I knew these people had education—something I didn't have. I went to school very sporadically as a young person. Just enough to learn the bare basics of reading and writing. I ended up teaching myself more of the three Rs by necessity. Those people up on Mount Morris had solid educations, which gave them a hell of a lot more options than I had. Their proper way of dressing, walking, and talking made them nearly invisible to me.

The underworld was in full, living color. The prostitutes and their pimps, the numbers runners and their clients, the drug dealers and, most especially, the gamblers, who always had lots of money. They spoke a language I could read, write, and understand fluently.

The underworld was going to be how I made my living. Just didn't know for sure what my specialty would be. I knew I wasn't going to be a pimp. Never liked pimps. Still don't. If you gotta make your money off a woman's body, you should just go ahead and kill yourself. That's how I feel about that. I ain't never getting my money off a woman's ass. Never. So that was out. You needed some kind of connection to get into numbers running. I knew how to rob a numbers runner. But I didn't know how to get my own spot—or if I really wanted to do that. I was too wild at that time to settle down and do something like run a numbers spot. I wanted fast money. I wanted to work independently. And I wanted my money in a hurry.

A few months after I started stealing anything not nailed down in Harlem, I was introduced to the heroin trade. I'd met a guy named Fletcher. We started small-talking at a hot-dog stand over on 116th and 8th Avenue and I mentioned something about a man named MP, a cousin of my daddy's.

Fletcher said, "MP! From down North Carolina?"

Turns out he was related to MP, too. Fletcher gave me a big old hug and we laughed about the coincidence of distant relatives meeting up in Harlem at a hot-dog stand. I wasn't doing so bad at the time, and I remember I gave Fletcher a five-dollar bill that day. And ever since that day, whenever I ran into him, he was on me like stink on shit.

Fletcher was a junkie. A heroin addict. And he was my first real introduction to that whole world. I started running into Fletcher and his junkie friends here and there. And it always made me sick to my stomach, watching them ease those needles into their arms. They looked sick, desperate, and pathetic. I thought it was the worst thing ever.

"Yeah, it ain't good," Fletcher told me one day, after he hit me up for a few dollars. "But you could make some money selling it."

I'd already seen how the junkies, no matter how bad they looked, always managed to have enough money to buy whatever they needed. Although I thought junkies were pathetic, if they would help my money grow, I'd deal with it.

I started watching the streets more carefully, seeing the heroin dealers and how they came out in the morning, passed off the tiny glassine envelopes for a few hours—and then disappeared.

The men I saw worked quickly, worked alone, and the traffic of customers coming up to them provided a steady influx of cash. I wanted in.

"Who do I see about getting in on this?" I asked Fletcher one night.

"Old Man Pop would probably sell you enough to get started."

"Where would I find him?"

"Down on One Hundred Sixteenth Street. Jim Dandy's bar."

I went by there with a friend named Jerry, a guy I'd met through Fletcher. Jerry knew Old Man Pop and I knew I'd need someone to introduce me to him. You can't just walk up to a supplier and tell him you want to buy. Even if he knows your face, someone's got to vouch for you.

I met Jerry at the bar and we walked down to where Old

Man Pop was standing behind the bar, rinsing out glasses and putting them away.

"You got anything?" Jerry asked him.

"What do you want?" Old Man Pop asked.

Jerry pointed to me. "He wants it."

"How much?"

"Half an ounce."

"Come back in forty-five minutes," he said.

We left, and I went back with three hundred dollars and bought my first half ounce of heroin. He slid it to me in a brown paper bag right there on the bar.

Somebody—I can't remember who but it was probably my cousin Fletcher—had already shown me how to prepare the heroin for street sale. How to sift it a few times and weaken it a bit with a combination of quinine and something we called bonita, which was like powdered baby formula. Should be 60 percent heroin and 40 percent of the quinine and bonita mixture. Quinine was originally used for fevers. Eventually someone figured out that you could use it to cut heroin, too.

I didn't even bother to go straight home after picking up my package from Old Man Pop. I had the nerve to stroll right into the closest pharmacy to pick up some quinine and bonita before I went home.

There's different kinds of heroin. Stuff from Thailand is yellow and fluffy. Mexico makes a mud-brown version. It's gonna look different depending on where you get it from. The stuff I got from Old Man Pop was white, which meant it was from somewhere in Europe. I went home and prepared my inventory, sifting, cutting, and bagging it up.

The next day, I went out for my first day at my new job.

It was a fall morning and the weather was cool. I put on my black leather suit, 'gator boots, and a black cowboy hat.

After three hours, I had nine hundred dollars. Triple what I'd given Old Man Pop. Before the afternoon was over, I was back in that bar.

"Let me get a full ounce," I told Old Man Pop, sliding six hundred dollars over the counter.

"Come back in an hour," he said.

I went home, cut my stuff, packaged it, and hit the street the next morning at ten. By six that night, I was sold out again. I went straight back to the bar. But Old Man Pop wasn't there. If he would have been there, I would have hit the street that very night. I had to wait until the next morning. I went back and got two ounces. From then on, I tried to double whatever I got from Old Man Pop. Sometimes I went back twice in a day to re-up.

The money started coming in quick. Faster than robbing people. And with much less energy. I wasn't running from people. I didn't have to be violent or get into any kind of physical altercation. All I had to do was prepare my packages, go outside, and wait for my customers to come to me. And, of course, look out for Johnny Law.

The three hundred dollars I made the first night became three thousand dollars a night within a week. It was almost too easy. It was easy enough to turn my attention to the women Harlem had to offer. When I first got up there, I messed around with a few women here and there. But until I was making some real money, I wasn't really doing that much in that department.

After the money started coming in, I started getting my social life together. First, I got a new apartment overlooking

Central Park on Seventh Avenue. It was a one-bedroom with a little kitchenette. I was on the sixteenth floor of a high-rise. Big picture windows overlooking the park. Rent was a hundred dollars a month. And a fifty-dollar bill answered all questions about where I got my money.

It was furnished, but I didn't like any of the stuff in there so I got rid of it all. I bought a leather couch and chairs for the living room. I picked out my own chandelier that cost me ninety dollars. Which was a hell of a lot of money back then. I had been walking on Twenty-third Street and Second Avenue, passed a lighting shop, and I saw the chandelier and it just caught my eye so I bought it and had them come and install it.

I was tall and skinny and handsome. Had leather outfits in different colors, down and Izod jackets from fancy department stores.

Needless to say, I had plenty of women in New York City falling over my shoes. And it was women of all ages. The older women had no idea that the man who took them out and later took them home was only a teenager.

One day, I was over on 114th Street and 8th Avenue. I had a friend named Rev who used to wash cars around there. By this point, I had a Cadillac convertible—red exterior, black leather interior. And Rev always took good care of my ride. He invited me out to his place, where he lived with his old lady. When I went out there, his wife's niece was visiting.

Now, this young lady was a real country girl, reminded me of the girls back home. I could tell she wasn't fast or worldly. She was a real old-school country girl. I stood in front of Rev's building and watched his niece walk toward me, on her way home from work.

"What's your name?" I asked.

"Annabelle," she said.

"Annabelle, I'm Frank Lucas."

"Nice to meet you, Mr. Lucas."

She had a deep Southern accent just like mine, a quiet voice, and a shy smile.

"You ain't from around here, are you?" I asked.

"Nah, sir, I ain't. Just came up from down South for a job."

"That so?"

"Yes, sir, it is."

I walked over to my convertible and opened the passenger's side door.

"Let's go, Annabelle."

"'Scuse me?"

"Now don't talk back to me, Annabelle," I said with a smile. "I don't like that. When I tell you to do something, I expect you to do it."

"Yes, sir," Annabelle said, slipping into the soft leather of my car and looking up at me with a nervous look on her face.

"You with Frank Lucas today, no need in looking nervous. I ain't gon' let nothin' happen to you. Lest you want it to."

Now I gotta tell you about Annabelle. She wasn't a pretty girl. She was short and had a plain, round face. Pretty good head of hair. But she had a real nice shape. Real nice. But she wasn't as pretty as a lot of the girls I was running around with. There was something else about Annabelle. Maybe she reminded me of home. I don't know. But I liked her right away. Could've been just that body of hers.

I took her to Baby Grand. That night, Nipsey Russell and

Pigmeat Markman were performing. After the show, I was planning to take her right back to Rev's house. But I pulled up to my apartment building real quick to get something and told Annabelle to wait in the car.

"I'll come up with you," she said.

I did a double-take and saw that Annabelle had let her dress slip up a certain way, giving me a good look at her thoroughbred thighs. I double parked the car and went upstairs with Annabelle. She went and took a shower and came out wearing one of my dress shirts unbuttoned.

Let me tell you something. I'm seventy-seven years old right now telling this story. And my legs are shaking just thinking about what Annabelle did to me that night. And it was sixty years ago. Anabelle was something else. She was a good country girl everywhere but in the bed. I didn't leave my apartment for two days. By the time I came out to take her back to Rev's place, I had five tickets on my car and it was still double-parked on the street.

I continued to see Annabelle here and there. Of course, I messed with a lot of women, some of the baddest women in New York City. Everybody wanted my women—except for Annabelle. She didn't look worth a shit. But I had love for her.

I was on the streets every morning, selling the heroin I was buying in larger and larger quantities from Old Man Pop. I would come home with my pockets bulging with cash, wrinkled singles, five and twenty dollar bills. The more I sold, the more money I made. The more I made, the more I bought. The more I bought, the more I sold. It didn't seem like the cycle had a cap at all. I bought a second Cadillac, a sky blue convertible with white interior.

I was really doing it now. I'd done a complete 180 from my life running from the Klan down south. It had only been a year. But those memories seemed like someone else's lifetime. Felt like I was sitting on top of the world.

And then I ran into Diggs and Pappo. The two men who would make my life miserable for the next two years.

3

In the underworld environment, cops are the natural enemy of a drug dealer. It was my job to just stay out of their way. But that rule only applies to cops trying to do their job. Crooked cops have no rules and no ethics. And some of them get a badge just so they can have a license to beat people up and rob them.

If I ever turned a corner and saw Diggs and his partner, Pappo, my stomach sank and my temper jumped a few degrees.

"If it isn't Frank Lucas," Diggs would say, grabbing me by my collar. Diggs was six foot five, at least three hundred pounds. Muscles like Hulk Hogan's. He was twice as big as I was. Don't ask me why he was always picking on me.

"You got a reason to have your hands on me?" I'd say.

"We can make one up if you don't shut the fuck up," Pappo would chime in.

Diggs and Pappo would take me behind a building and punch me in my stomach and face, for no good reason except that they could.

"We heard someone snatched some chains over on Lexington and One Hundred Sixteenth," said Diggs, before socking me in the jaw. "Was it you?"

"No, it wasn't!' I said, rubbing my chin. "You see any chains on me?"

"What's this?" said Pappo, putting his hands in my pocket and pulling out a gold chain.

"Get the fuck out of here," I said. "You just put that in there."

"Let's go, Lucas."

I would struggle all the way into the police car. Because I knew that once they got me to the precinct, it was really over. They'd work me over with rubber hoses, their fists and legs, until they were too tired to beat my ass anymore. Then they'd throw me out of the station and I'd look like I just came out of a grinding machine, bloody and swollen.

Except for Diggs and Pappo, things were sweet for me. Had a nice place, more money than I could spend, and any woman I wanted at my fingertips. I was coming home and throwing my money into dresser drawers around my apartment. I didn't put any of it in the bank. I just threw it wherever and took out whatever I needed. I wasn't organized or thinking ahead. I was just keeping one foot in front of the other and surviving.

At one point, I took an afternoon off to count up all the money I had strewn around my place. I was curious about just how much I had. The money was flowing like water and I was losing touch with what it represented collectively. It's like if you leave the water running in your sink: if it goes right down the drain, you don't realize how much water you're wasting. But if you put a stopper in the sink and the water collects, you see how quickly it overflows and realize how much you've been wasting.

I counted, making thousand-dollar piles and stacking them around my apartment. When I was done, I had a half-million dollars.

I was stunned. I knew I'd been making a lot of money, but I had no idea it was quite that much. I thought it was time to give myself a few days off from the streets. I sent my parents some money. And then I headed down to a craps game. I bet ten thousand dollars and left there twenty thousand dollars richer.

I'd been playing craps for years. And I often had a winning streak that would piss the other players off, like when I got jumped after beating all those boys out in Kentucky. I learned to play pool when I was in Kentucky, too. And I swore up and down I could beat anybody. And most of the time, I did. Craps was about chance and pool was about skill. But if I put money down on either, I rarely lost.

Until, of course, I started losing. It wasn't often. But it was enough to make my money start dwindling. Today, I can't even imagine how a half-million dollars in 1948 started to slip away from me. But it did. And quickly. Six months after I counted out my money that day, I had $250,000. I was buying out the bar whenever I felt like it, betting larger and larger numbers on craps and pool games, and just throwing money away on God knows what. I was too young and ignorant to think about finding someone to put it in the bank for me, or buy a house or make some other kind of investment. I just spent and spent and spent. I'd crash my car, leave it right there, and go straight to the car dealer and buy a new one.

While my money was withering away, I saw more and more of Diggs and Pappo. If a little kid took a piece of candy from a corner store, they were looking for me.

"What the fuck y'all want from me now?" I said one morning when they yanked me up after I came out of a corner store.

"Let's go," said Pappo.

"What kind of bullshit is this?"

As soon as we walked in to the precinct: *BAM!* Pappo punched me right in the face and my nose started spurting blood. I dropped my head, and as soon as I did, Diggs punched me on the side of my head and blood started seeping out of my left ear. The whole world dipped to one side as I gritted my teeth, clutched my hands and arms to cover my vital organs, and tried to steel myself through the beat-down. They used their hands, feet, and a rubber hose to damn near kill me. It lasted for fifteen minutes. Just long enough for me to end up throwing up blood for the next three weeks.

When I got back uptown, I made a solemn vow to myself. I was never getting beat down by Diggs and Pappo again. Ever. The next time I saw them, one of us was going to die if they even *looked* like they wanted to put a hand on me.

Soon after that incident, my money dipped so low that I had to sell my red-and-black Cadillac just to keep up with my gambling debts and pay my measly one-hundred-dollar-a-month rent. A few months after that, I had to sell the sky-blue convertible. I kept shooting craps. And of course, when you really need to win, you lose.

It got so bad that I got a notice that I was being evicted.

I gathered up what I could carry in a single bag and walked out of my first decent apartment and never looked back. Left all the furniture I'd bought and that fancy chandelier.

I tried to get back in the game selling heroin. But I owed a few dealers money and no one would front me a supply. I was flat broke and homeless. Now I'd done a 360-degree turn from my days in North Carolina. The only difference was that I wasn't in La Grange. I was in Harlem, a place where you get nothing but second chances.

I tried to get back to selling drugs steadily. Finally got someone to front me some product. And then I ended up getting arrested and sent to The Tombs, the downtown jail at 125 White Street, for nine months. It was my first serious arrest and, besides little stints here and there, it was my first real jail sentence. I was still messing with Annabelle and she still had that little job making sixty dollars a week. She'd come downtown to The Tombs and bring me cigarettes and shit. She was the only person I wanted to see down there. I didn't tell any of my other associates.

I had nine months in The Tombs to think. Nine months to get my mind right. Takes nine months for a child to be ready to leave its momma's womb. Turns out I needed those nine months to be reborn.

I wish I could say that after I got out of The Tombs, I had my mind straight and had a plan that made sense. Instead, I went back to the first job I had when I came to Harlem— robbing and stealing.

By this time, people knew my name and my face, so going back to my old profession probably wasn't the smartest move. But of course, I didn't give a good goddamn. I needed money and I was going to get it however I had to. Numbers runners, store owners, and whoever else had anything for me to take got robbed before they knew it was coming. If I had to knock you upside the head, I did it. If I could just snatch the money out of your hands, even better. I got more daring and less careful. And I began to rack up enemies who were out there looking for me faster than I was getting money.

Two enemies that I finally got rid of were the two cops, Diggs and Pappo. One day, soon after robbing a bodega, I was walking up Eighth Avenue on my way to get something to eat. I was always on alert, my eyes darting every which way whenever I was on the streets. I heard a car slow up behind me and waited briefly before turning around. It was Diggs and Pappo.

"Frank, where you been?" said Diggs.

I felt my blood start boiling. If either one of them wanted to start with me, I was ready. I had a .45 on me. And I knew in that moment that if they touched me, I was going to kill them both, right there in broad daylight. If I got locked up, so be it. There was no way I was letting them disrespect me again.

I kept walking. But I didn't increase my speed. I was just waiting for them to start fucking with me.

"Frank, you hear me talking to you?!" Diggs said.

The car was cruising slowly enough to not pass me as I walked. I put my hand on my gun, which was tucked into my waistband. Finally, I stopped. I heard the car stop behind me.

"I'll tell y'all motherfuckers something right now," I said, staring them both down. "It's a real good goddamned day to die."

I don't know what came over me. But I wasn't getting beat up by them again. Diggs and Pappo must have known that I felt like I had nothing to lose, because they both looked at me for a long second. And then they pulled off and kept driving up Eighth Avenue. I never saw either of them again.

I was now free to continue in my life of crime without any interruptions. After robbing a few numbers runners, I went up to A. J. Lester's, a clothing store on 125th Street and 8th Avenue, to get my wardrobe back together. It was early in the morning when I went in and I noticed right away that they had only two employees, a salesman on the floor and a manager I could hear on the phone in a back office. I picked out a few items, and as I paid for my new threads, I was also casing the joint.

A few days later, I came in, right at ten when they opened up. There were two salesmen on the floor. If there had been a woman working that morning, I would have walked right up out of there. I wouldn't rob no spot with a woman working—no way. I had my .45 at my hip, but I knew I wasn't going to have any problems.

"Give me the shit. Now," I said to the tall, red-complexioned guy who was manning the floor. I slipped the .45 out of my waistband just enough for him to see what I was working with.

"Don't want no problems," he said, hustling over to the cash register and stabbing at the keys.

"That makes two of us," I said. "Move faster."

I kept one eye on the door and one on the man emptying the register. I stuffed my bag with the money and dashed out. They didn't even follow me out of the store or yell for help. I went to my car parked around the corner and drove downtown to Fifty-seventh Street to chill out for a minute. Ended up picking up a white girl and laying up in a hotel in midtown for a week or so.

Don't remember how much money I got from A. J. Lester's. A few hundred dollars. I remember thinking that the whole thing went well—except it was a Wednesday. I was a damn fool, robbing them in the middle of the week. I should've waited until the end of the week, when they would have had more money in the store. The two or three hundred I got was probably just what they got from the bank to make change.

The next week, I hit up a small grocery store on 141st and 8th Avenue. They had collard greens and other vegetables set up in the front of the store. I had come by a few times and noticed a manager handing over money to a delivery truck. Like most stores in Harlem, it was owned by a Jewish guy and run by a few black folks. I drove over one morning, parked around the corner, and made my way inside. I didn't bother with the cashiers this time. I went straight back to the manager's office. (All managers' offices are situated in the exact same spot in these kinds of stores. You follow the aisles leading to a back entrance. There'll be a hallway where deliveries will come in. Probably a bathroom on one side. And the other side will almost always be the manager's office.) I barged in and then stood behind him where he couldn't see me.

"Act busy," I said, the pistol pressed to his back.

"What do you want?" he said. I could see his white skin turning pink.

"What you think I want?" I asked. "Give me whatever you got in here."

The manager reached over to the lock box and took out the money with one hand, transferred it to his other hand, and put it on his desk right next to where I stood.

"You come out after me and I'll kill you," I said as I left his office.

Can't tell you how much I got from that job, so don't ask me. But it wasn't enough. I can tell you that. It wasn't enough to get me back in the game the way I had been before. I needed a car (or two). I wasn't living the lifestyle that Harlem had shown me was possible. I had to get more daring, more I-don't-give-a-fuck. And for me, that was not a problem at all.

Although I was doing all kinds of dirt in New York City, I still managed to get back down to North Carolina to see my family whenever I could.

In 1947, I had gone down for a visit, while the cops were looking for me up North for a robbery and I needed to cool my heels out of town. While I was there, I met up with Flora, a country girl with a cute smile and a great pair of legs. We had a good time while I was at home, but I went back to New York thinking that would be the extent of our relationship.

And then I got word that Flora was pregnant. I came back to North Carolina and ended up taking her to the hospital when she went into labor. Back then, you couldn't find out ahead of time which gender you were having. I didn't care one way or another. I was young. Wasn't even sure if I was ready to be a father. I hung around the hospital while I waited to hear back from the doctor.

"Girls," the doctor said.

"It's a girl?"

"Two girls," he said.

I almost passed out. Twins? We had no idea. We named our daughters Betty and Ruby Lucas. Flora was still young, living with her parents and all that. I never gave a second thought to building a life in North Carolina. I'm sorry to say it, but that just wasn't what was in the cards for me. I wanted them to have a good life and I knew I'd do the best I could to provide for them. But I knew that unless they moved up North, I was not going to be a regular presence in their lives.

Now, I was a father. And I was also a die-hard criminal. For a while, I was ten times better as a criminal than I was as a father. Soon after my twin daughters were born, I was back in New York, tearing things up and making money at the same time.

4

With the money I got from a grocery-store robbery, I went down to Bush Jewelers on 125th between Seventh and Lenox Avenues to get myself a new watch. I'd been running a scam on them for a while. I'd go in with fake ID, get something on credit, and never go back to pay for it. Go back in again with another fake ID, walk out with something else, and never make any payments.

I went in to pick out a watch, and as the salesman brought out different choices, I looked around and saw that they had no security guards. Immediately, I knew I was coming back the next day to hit them up. Now, Bush Jewelers was a big store, not one of the two-bit storefronts that lined Seventh Avenue. This was the big time. It was only one floor but it was wide. As I looked over the tray of watches the salesman brought to me, I noticed that there were two main counters that lined the side walls of the store and one counter in the middle of the store. There were men lined up behind both counters. I knew when I came back I wasn't going to go too far away from that front door. So I planned to hit up one of the men positioned closest to the entrance. I didn't get the watch on credit. I bought it with cash. I knew I was getting it back very soon.

The next day, I drove to the store, parked around the corner, and made sure I was ready. I didn't bring my .45. I knew I wouldn't need it. And you never bring a weapon unless you have to. This was not going to be a violent, strong-arm robbery. And by the looks of the salesmen they had working in the store, I just knew it wasn't necessary. All I took with me was a small leather valise to drop the jewels in.

When I got to the entrance, I took a split second to decide if I would go to the man on my left or the one on my right. The man to my left was wearing thick Coke-bottle eyeglasses. I went for him. He looked like he was too blind to see his hands in front of him.

"I need to see some loose diamonds," I said. I took out a knot of cash. "I'm setting a diamond into an engagement ring."

"Well, congratulations!" the man said. He slid out a tray of loose diamonds.

I knew I couldn't be bothered with a bunch of jewelry already set into necklaces and rings. Too hard to sell and not as valuable as loose diamonds. I looked over the tray he brought out, comparing a few diamonds.

"One of these could work. But I was looking for a blue diamond."

"We have those, too, sir," he said. He was staring so hard at my thick knot of cash that he foolishly brought out another tray without putting the first tray back. He didn't see that all I had was six hundred-dollar bills wrapped up around a bunch of cut-up newspaper. He also didn't see the bag I had open and ready tucked under the counter.

As soon as he sat the second tray down at the counter, I snatched both trays and dumped them into my bag, turned on my heel, and ran out. I heard a gunshot as soon as I ran up the street and I kept running another half block before I dipped into a doorway. I listened. I heard no sirens. I peeked out. No cops coming in my direction. No one chasing me. I hailed a cab and went home.

I asked around to figure out how I could get a decent price for my diamonds. Someone told me about a guy named Cool Breeze who would be able to take the diamonds off my hands. I met up with him at Adel's Kitchen, a restaurant on Seventh Avenue.

"Thirty thousand," he said. "More if you can wait a few days."

I didn't have time to wait for anything.

"I'll take it now," I said, handing over the bag for him to inspect the goods.

Frank Lucas was back in business. And this time, I knew I was not going to lose my money playing craps or slipping up and enjoying the money too much to keep bringing it in. That would never happen to me again. Even though my money was getting back to where it needed to be, I still wasn't satisfied. And I was so reckless, I didn't care where the next payout came from.

Cool Breeze handed over my cash and I couldn't help but wonder. Where did he get that kind of money? And how could I find more people like him that had that kind of money?

My answer was in a place called The Big Track.

The Big Track was a big-time gambling spot in the basement of a large high-rise apartment building on 145th Street near St. Nicholas. This was a spot where losing twenty grand on a game was nothing. There were five or six craps tables in there and always at least ten or fifteen guys inside. Hundreds of thousands of dollars went in and out of those doors on a daily basis. I never played. I just went in a few times and hung out with a few people I'd met on the street. One of 'em was a guy named Johnny. I can't say he was a real friend, 'cause I didn't have any real friends back then. Ain't so sure I have any real friends today. But back then, we'd started running the streets together and we ended up hanging out at The Big Track a few times.

You'd walk into the building on the ground floor, go up a few steps, and then ring a doorbell. They had a doorman who'd let you in, and you'd go in and win or lose your money. Might be a woman or two in there. Had a small bar in the corner. Nothing fancy. But it didn't need to be. Not with all that money changing hands.

"Who's that?" I said to Johnny one night, nodding toward a thin man with small, beady eyes.

"That's Wynton," he said. "Wynton Morris. That dude standing next to him? They call him Fat Daddy."

"And that's Cool Breeze next to him, right?"

"Yeah, that's him."

I kept my eyes on the knot of money in his hands.

"Who is that?" I asked Johnny, jutting my chin toward a man standing near Cool Breeze and laughing out loud.

"Lil' Man," Johnny said, shaking his head slowly. "I'm telling you, Frank, these niggas ain't no joke."

I just nodded my head and kept my eyes wide open. They should have had better security in there. 'Cause once I saw the kind of money they were working with in there, I knew The Big Track was going to be my next target.

It was July. Hot as hell outside and I was wearing a coat, as usual. For two reasons. First, I was used to wearing a coat just in case I had to end up sleeping outside, in a doorway or in a park. From my early days of being on the run, I'd gotten used to keeping a coat with me all the time. And even after I got a piece-of-shit room at a boardinghouse, I usually wore my coat everywhere.

It also was a good cover for my two guns: a .45 semi-automatic and a .44 magnum revolver. And on that sweltering July afternoon, I had both my guns under my coat as I walked up to The Big Track. The doorman, recognizing me from the few times I came in with Johnny, let me right on in. I stood near the door and watched for ten minutes. I can't remember everyone who was in The Big Track that day. But I do know there were a lot of the usual suspects; a few of the guys Johnny had pointed out to me were hunched over the craps tables, placing bets and yelling exclamations when the dice hit the tables.

Finally, after I surveyed the scene, I opened up my coat and took out my revolver.

"Y'all motherfuckers know what this is," I screamed. "Up against the wall."

The group of men went quiet and looked over at me. I had my gun cocked and I was ready to shoot.

"Are you crazy?" one guy asked.

"Up against the wall," I said. "Or I'ma show you just crazy I am."

A few men shook their heads in disbelief as they lined up against the wall behind the craps table.

"Clothes off," I screamed. "Get 'em off fast. And you—"

I pointed my gun at Cool Breeze. "Throw all them pants to the middle of the floor or I'll blow your fucking head off."

You gotta understand, what I was doing was absolutely unheard of. You could take your chances on robbing random people in Harlem, but you did not rob a place like The Big Track. It was like robbing the Italian mafia. You just didn't do it. There were too many bad-asses with too many connections to even dream about messing with them and their money. But I didn't care one whit about any of that.

I needed money. And I knew these fools had it. And I'm telling you right now, I was prepared to kill any of them if they got in the way of what I was there to do.

The men in the basement were peeling off their pants and throwing them to Cool Breeze, who was throwing them in my direction. One guy, the one they called Fat Daddy, was grumbling.

"I ain't taking off shit," he said. "I don't give a fuck what this dude is talking about."

"I told you twice," I said. "I ain't telling you a third time."

"This nigga must be crazy!" Fat Daddy said.

I pointed my gun in his direction and squeezed off a shot. *"Pop!"*

I capped Fat Daddy right in his ass and he started wailing.

"Anybody else got some shit to say?"

It was quiet. I rifled through the pockets of the pants Cool Breeze had thrown in my direction, grabbed all the cash inside, and stuffed it into my pockets.

"Come after me and I'll blow your head off," I said, backing up toward the door.

I walked out backward and then ran out of the building and down the street. Like always, I ran for a few blocks and then started walking when I knew I wasn't being chased. I went to the rooming house to count my money. It was almost fifteen thousand dollars.

And I knew it wasn't anywhere near all the money they had in there. If I'd taken someone with me who could have kept an eye on everyone while I went through their pockets and the whole spot more thoroughly, I know I could have gotten ten times that amount. I put the bulk of my money up, peeled off some for myself, and went straight to The Hideout, my favorite bar on 113th Street and 8th Avenue.

"What you getting?" the bartender asked as I sat on the stool, my pockets bulging with cash.

"Give me a shot of Dewar's," I said. "And set up a round for everybody in here!"

A few hours later, Johnny came and sat next to me at the bar.

"You gotta get out of town, Frank. Fast."

I drained my drink and kept my eye on a pretty young thing on the other side of the bar.

"Why's that?"

"Cool Breeze and Fat Daddy and all of them. They describing you to everyone in Harlem. Just a matter of time before they catch up to you. And they'll kill you, Frank. I heard Winty put out the word to kill you on sight."

I nodded.

"So are you going?" Johnny asked. "Are you gonna leave town?"

"My name is Frank Lucas," I said. "And I don't run."

For the next few weeks, I was on high alert. I pulled out

my gun if I even thought someone was giving me a second glance. I didn't keep any kind of routine and never slept in the same place two nights in a row.

If Cool Breeze and the rest of them were looking for me, I couldn't tell. Because as I spent their money in every bar and diner in Harlem, no one stepped to me.

Looking back, I think they were waiting to see what my deal was. Later on, I'd experience the same thing with guys that were as crazy as I was. Years later, a guy named Tango would pull some similar shit, letting me know he was just crazy. But you had to take some time before you went after these types. Because if they were truly crazy, they'd come out, guns blazing, and kill anyone and everyone without thinking twice about it. Those types might start a shootout in the street in the middle of the day, hit some women and kids. Next thing you know, the cops are swarming in to take everybody down. Those real crazy types you had to keep an eye on for a minute. Watch 'em. Research their moves. See if they were working for somebody else. You'd have to catch them at just the right place and time. Or who knows what would happen.

I think that's why Cool Breeze and the rest of them didn't come at me right away. Anyone as crazy as I was, who would rob them with no mask and no backup, had to be crazy. And I think they were mulling over how to handle me with the least amount of drama.

They were right: I *was* crazy. I didn't care about anything except where my next dollar was coming from and how I was going to spend it. After the robbery, I bought myself a car, got another apartment and a whole new wardrobe. I bought a bunch of new suits from Phil Kronfeld's on Forty-ninth and Broadway. I was back to living the high life, while half of Harlem was grumbling about me and wanted me dead or locked up. I heard through the grapevine that I had at least five contracts out on my life. From the grocery-store owner to the group of gangsters I'd robbed at the gambling spot, people were straight up making deals and promising money to anyone who would kill me dead in the street.

I should mention here that I was all of seventeen years old.

I wasn't afraid to die. More than that, I just didn't care about dying. I was young, tough, good-looking, and strong. I was prepared to do whatever I had to do to live. If that meant killing anyone who tried to kill me, so be it.

For several weeks, I was a wanted man. But if you'd run into me at one of my Harlem hangouts you'd never have known it by looking at me. I was calm, cool, and collected. I woke up every morning ready to kill on sight. I may not have realized it then, but looking back, my days were numbered. I was two seconds away from killing someone and going to jail for a very long time or being killed myself.

I continued robbing whoever and wherever, getting my money up, and I was still dating any woman I wanted. There was this girl named Jesse who used to always be at Ma Belle's, a bar with a kitchen on 114th Street and 8th Avenue. Now, Jesse was a good-looking girl, light skinned with a face full of freckles. She was five foot five with a shape you could take to the pawnshop. I got tired of seeing her up in Ma Belle's and not being on my arm. I started taking her out here and there, fitting her in between my other women. About a month after we started seeing each other, I saw her at Ma Belle's at the counter and grabbed her up by her arm.

"Let's go, Jesse," I said. "I'm taking you home with me."

"Not tonight, Frank," she said, looking nervously around the restaurant.

"Woman, don't you know you can't say no to me?"

"Frank, I gotta tell you something."

"You ain't gotta tell me nothing but you ready to go."

Jesse grabbed my hand and forced me to sit on a stool at the counter next to her.

"Frank. My old man heard we've been seeing each other."

"I don't give a fuck about your man," I said. "He ain't got nothing to do with me."

"I just don't know if—"

Jesse stopped talking and I turned to follow her line of vision. A tall, thin man with wide, bulging eyes came striding over to where we sat. And *pow!*—he slapped Jesse upside the head and she went right to the floor.

"What's wrong with you?" I said, as a few women scrambled to pick Jesse up and take her behind the counter.

"Ain't nobody talking to you!" he said.

"Why don't you pick on someone your own fucking size?" I said, standing up.

"You my size!" the man said. Then he made a grave mistake and snatched me up by the collar.

That's a real disrespectful motion right there. Grabbing a man by the collar like he's a child. Or a dog. I've never been able to contain my temper when a grown man treats me like I'm a child or an animal. Back then, I had no control over my temper. I could go from zero to sixty in one second flat. I didn't even have time to think about what I wanted to do. When that fool grabbed my shirt collar, I punched him directly in the face and heard him squeal like a little girl.

"Yeah, you my size, right?" I asked, barreling into him with my fists, hearing him scream louder each time. "You still want to fuck with me?" I said, kicking, punching, and slapping him until I saw blood coming out of different parts of his body. I was hitting and kicking him so hard that I heard him begging me to stop. But I couldn't. He'd already come in there acting like he was the man. And I couldn't rein in my temper, even after I saw that he had given up. He soiled himself and started vomiting, which made everyone in the restaurant run out screaming and covering their mouths.

I came out of the trance and saw Jesse's man crumpled in a ball on the floor.

"My name is Frank Lucas," I said in a calm voice. "Don't ever disrespect me. Ever."

I added another person to the lengthy list of people who wanted me dead. They say that God looks after babies and fools. I was neither. But I guess God looks after criminals with bad tempers, too. Because at the moment I walked out of Ma Belle's and headed back to my place, I was a man marked for death. And somehow, for some reason I still don't understand sixty years later, a man was sent into my life who would end up saving me from sure death.

5

I think we need to recap right here before I go any further. I come up to Harlem in the mid-1940s, just barely a teenager. I start robbing and stealing, move on to selling heroin, and within a few years, I'd made and lost hundreds of thousands of dollars. And it wasn't from the stock market or some other kind of way that makes you feel disconnected from the cash. This was cash, crumpled bills fished out of the pockets of junkies, crisp bills that janitors and teachers brought straight from the bank. This was the money of the masses, filtering its way through my pockets. And I took it straight to the gambling and pool halls throughout my neighborhood and lost every penny.

So, I went back to robbing and stealing. And I ended up two seconds away from getting my head blown off by any number of people in Harlem who wanted me dead. I was on borrowed time.

I was trying to move out of robbing and stealing and look for another way to get my money. I always made sure to read the newspaper every day and I watched the news every night. It was a habit I'd started as soon as I came to New York. It always seemed to me that if you just paid attention to what was going on in the world, you could learn something about what your own next step should be. Many a night, I sat in a pool hall or at a bar, staring up at the evening news or flipping through the newspaper.

One day, I read about a killing that had taken place in midtown Manhattan. Someone a reporter called "Icepick Red" was sticking an ice pick into the chests of people and walking on down the street minding his business. He'd be away from the scene damn near before the victim hit the ground.

I knew Icepick Red. Well, I didn't know him, but I knew *of* him. I saw him slinking around Harlem. Icepick was a nasty motherfucker. Always walking down the street, spitting on the ground without even looking to see who might be nearby. He was tall—at least six foot four—and skinny as a rail and so light he looked like a white boy. The rumor on the streets was that people who needed someone killed went to see Icepick Red. For twenty-five thousand dollars, he'd take care of it. I wondered if I was worth that much. Would one of the gangsters I'd robbed at The Big Track pay Icepick Red twenty-five thousand dollars to kill me? I doubted it. They could find and kill me themselves if they really wanted to.

But beyond that, I wondered if Icepick needed a little help in the kill-for-hire business. I would have killed someone for twenty-five thousand dollars. Without thinking twice about it. It's the mind frame I was in at the time. I was an animal, a beast. It was kill or be killed, as far as I was concerned. And since I was marked for death anyway, I didn't see anything wrong with killing for a living. I made up my mind to approach Icepick Red the next time I saw him, just to see if I could get him to talk to me. I wanted to know how he got his assignments. All I knew was that he was killing guineas downtown. And he had no crew. Nothing but him.

A few weeks later and I see his long, skinny frame ambling up Eighth Avenue. I'm leaning up against a building, reading the paper about another victim found in midtown with an ice pick sticking straight out of his chest.

"How you doing, sir?" I asked, as he came closer to where I stood.

Icepick Red coughed up a mouthful of phlegm and spit it out, just missing where I stood. That was all Icepick Red had to say to me. But we'd end up meeting again soon.

"Any punk in here want to play some fucking pool? A thousand or get the fuck out my face."

I was at Metin's Pool Room at 118th and 7th Avenue. It was a dreary, rainy Saturday morning. The streets were still being watched, so I hadn't pulled off a good heist in a while, and I was doing bad. No place to stay, no clothes, nothing. I'd started hustling pool and gambling as my source of income. It wasn't steady work. Sometimes you're flush, sometimes you're dead-ass broke. That night, I was dead-ass broke.

I was watching a few pool games, hoping I could get in on something, when Icepick Red came in and yelled out his challenge. The pool hall was loud and crowded, dozens of people hunched over several pool tables, smoking, drinking, yelling, and cursing. A few people turned to look at Icepick Red but no one took him up on his offer. Icepick Red looked down at me, the only person staring at him right in the face.

"Fuck you looking at?" He spat. "Somebody playing or what?"

"I ain't got but three dollars," I said.

"That's what's wrong with all you punks," Icepick Red said. "I should shoot all of y'all for coming in here with no fucking money."

Icepick put his hand on his waistband and a few more people took their eyes away from their game and eyed Icepick.

"That's all the money I got," I said.

I didn't take my eyes off him. I wasn't scared of him. Not one iota. I knew I could beat his ass in pool. He could shoot me, sure. But so the fuck what? Kill me. Or don't. Whatever. Back in Kentucky, the old men who had taught me to shoot pool told me that the game began before you even picked up your stick. You needed to believe you could beat somebody. And act like it. No room for fear.

"A thousand. Or get the fuck out of here," he said.

Icepick dragged his eyes around the room, silently threatening everyone in the pool hall. Some people continued darting their eyes in his direction. Some went back to their games. The music from the jukebox came back on loud and strong.

Then, the door to the pool hall opened, letting in a bit of the light from outside. And everything went dead quiet. Someone even turned the music off. You could hear a mouse piss on cotton in China. For some reason, I even felt something like fear course through me, and I didn't even know who was at the door. But I could tell that everyone in there was frozen and staring at the figure standing behind Icepick Red.

"Can you beat him?" I heard a voice behind Icepick Red ask me.

"Yes, sir, I can," craning my neck to see who was speaking.

The man was five foot nine, looked to be about 160 pounds. He had a round, brown-skinned face and a receding hairline. He was wearing a dark blue suit—looked like it cost more than the building we all stood in. I can see him right now, in my mind's eye. With a red rose in his lapel, same exact color as his red tie. Looked like something out of *Esquire* or *GQ*. I heard someone behind me whisper, "Bumpy Johnson . . ."

I'd never seen him before. But anyone living in Harlem knew the name Bumpy Johnson. I'd read his name in the paper a few times and I knew that if anyone in Harlem wanted to do any kind of big business, he had to come see Bumpy Johnson first. Or die.

I'd only been in New York for a few months, less than a year. And although I'd seen or met most of the underworld figures, I wasn't in deep enough to ever see someone like Bumpy Johnson. He was a *boss*. You didn't cross paths with him unless he wanted you to.

I only knew the basics about Bumpy, stuff I'd heard in the streets. He was from South Carolina. And I'd heard that he wasn't a typical gangster. He worked in the streets but he wasn't of the streets. He was refined and classy, more like a businessman with a legitimate career than most people in the underworld. I could tell by looking at him that he was a lot different from the people I saw in the streets.

"Lump, rack 'em up," Bumpy said to the man working the tables.

"I wasn't talking to you!" Icepick said, turning to face Bumpy.

Bumpy walked past Icepick a few steps and came to the pool table where I stood holding on to my cue stick.

"You can beat him, right?"

"Yes, sir."

Bumpy turned around.

"I said rack 'em up!"

Icepick mumbled and grumbled while Lump set up the balls. Meanwhile, every single person in that hall put their sticks down and crowded around the table where we were about to play. We shot to see who would get the first break. I broke first.

And the rest was history.

I remember that Howard Harrison, one of the few guys I was pretty cool with, stood behind me. Matter of fact, I've been looking for Howard ever since. We called him Boobie. Don't know if he's still out there but I sure would like to see him.

"Go 'head, Luke, get 'im," Howard said.

I ran the entire table. Bumped 'em perfect. I left Icepick's balls stacked together and I knew he wouldn't be able to break 'em up. And he didn't.

A few low whistles went up in the crowd when I was done. No one was cheering, though. Not with Icepick standing there, pissed off, his face beet red as he handed over the money to one of Bumpy Johnson's associates. Mr. Johnson exchanged a few quick pleasantries with some of the people in the pool hall, then he started walking toward the front door.

"Let's go, young man," he said to me.

I didn't think twice and followed him out of the bar. He had a Lincoln sedan with a driver idling outside the pool hall. I had no idea why this man in a flawless suit and fancy car had suddenly appeared in this hole in the wall or why he'd bet a thousand dollars that I could beat Icepick Red. Looking back, maybe Bumpy was just putting Icepick in his place. Or maybe he'd heard about this young punk robbing gangsters and ripping off everybody in Harlem and decided to deal with me. I have no idea. But when he waved a hand toward the backseat of his car, I got in with no hesitation.

"What's your name?" he asked.

"Frank Lucas."

"Where you living?"

"Ain't living nowhere right now."

"Where are your parents?"

"North Carolina. I came up here on my own."

"What you been doing for money?"

Something in Bumpy's face told me that I should be honest.

"Whatever I got to. Robbing. Stealing."

Bumpy nodded. "Imagine you got plenty of enemies behind that."

"Yes, sir, I do. I'm hearing a few people want me dead."

Bumpy raised his eyebrows. "That so? Who would that be?"

"Cool Breeze and them. I robbed them at The Big Track a while back."

"I see," he said.

Bumpy leaned up just a bit to speak with his driver. I couldn't hear what he told him. But the driver nodded and drove a few blocks east. We pulled up to The Big Track and

I wondered if he was planning to deliver me straight to the crew who wanted to kill me. When the car stopped Cool Breeze, Fat Daddy, and all the rest of them were standing right there, laughing and talking. They fell silent when the car pulled up.

Bumpy's driver came around and opened the door and Bumpy stepped out. He walked over to Cool Breeze and his crew, who were all now damn near at attention and ready to salute.

"You all see that young man in my car?" he asked.

Cool Breeze looked into the car without turning his head away from Bumpy.

"Yes, sir," he said.

"He works for me. Name is Frank Lucas. Leave him be. He works for me. Clear?"

"Yes, sir, Mr. Johnson," said Cool Breeze, while the other guys nodded and mumbled yessir and no problem, sir.

Bumpy held up a pointer finger. "Hands off," he said.

Bumpy got back in the car and tipped his hat to the guys standing on the street. He kept his eyes on the street ahead as the driver pulled away, but I couldn't help turning my head to look at the guys. They were still frozen, staring at Bumpy's car in shock.

"Who else?" he asked me.

"There's this guy . . . beat him up pretty bad at Ma Belle's . . ."

Bumpy took me with him to a few more places where I'd had trouble, from Bush Jewelers to a few corner stores. And each time, as soon as he walked in with me, everyone was all smiles and handshakes. I couldn't believe it. Store managers I'd help up at gunpoint were smiling in my face like I was their best friend. When we left the last spot, Bumpy again gestured for me to get in the backseat of the car.

"We're going to A. J. Lester's," Bumpy told his driver, who just nodded once.

At A. J. Lester's, Bumpy and I sat down while the salesman brought out racks and racks of clothing for me. Bumpy explained to me how suit pants should properly fall on a man's shoes, how his tie should look, the right way his hat should sit on his head, and how an overcoat should fit. I didn't say a word. I just nodded, listened, and said yessir if necessary.

His driver brought my bags into the car. Bumpy had bought me three suits, an overcoat, a few hats, dress shirts, and two pairs of Italian calf-leather shoes.

His driver pulled up to a house in Mount Morris Park, a classy part of Harlem I rarely had any business in.

It was a classic, well-kept brownstone on a leafy street. The first thing I noticed was how clean the neighborhood was. There was not a drop of trash or a stray piece of anything. His driver opened the heavy wood door and held it open for Mr. Johnson and me. There was a large foyer that led into a formally decorated parlor that looked like something I'd see in a magazine. Servants in uniform bustled about, taking Bumpy's coat, bringing him a drink, the evening papers, and filling him in on the events of the day at home.

"This way, Lucas," he told me, leading me up a flight of stairs.

He took me to the second floor, down a long corridor to a back bedroom.

"Here's where you'll stay tonight," he said. "In the morning, be ready at eight. You will come with me."

"Yessir."

I didn't feel comfortable sitting down while he was still standing in the doorway, glancing around the room. Finally, he tipped his head a bit and left the room, closing the door behind him. I still didn't feel comfortable sitting down. It was a queen-size bed, made up with fancy white linens that smelled like they'd been hung out to dry and then ironed crisp. There was artwork on the walls, depicting black people looking regal. It was like nothing I'd ever seen up close. And this was just one small, spare room in his house. It was better than entire apartments I'd lived in—even the fancy one with the chandelier I bought. It was clear that this man was refined. He had style. And he obviously had money. The little knick-knacks arranged on a bedside table looked like they'd cost a pretty penny. I sat down on the bed and exhaled.

Two hours before, I didn't know where my next meal was coming from and I was staring Icepick Red down, wondering if he was gonna shoot me for not having enough money to play him. And now I was in this man's well-appointed house. And he'd told all my enemies that I was now working for him.

I had no idea what this job would entail. But it didn't matter. If I found out the next day that I had to shoot people at point-blank range, I would have shrugged my shoulders and started firing.

From that day until the day he died, my place was at the right side of Bumpy Johnson. I went where he went. I did whatever he told me to do. I listened, I observed, and I learned. I didn't ask questions. I only followed commands and orders. And I learned everything about how the King of Harlem ran his enterprises.

For the first few months, my job consisted of sitting in the backseat of Bumpy's Lincoln and observing how he spent his days. He was an early riser. I always had to make sure I was up, showered, and dressed by eight. And no matter how early I got up and got dressed, Bumpy was already ready to go, sitting in the front parlor, reading the newspaper.

I started driving with Bumpy around to his usual spots, including breakfast and maybe a meeting in midtown Manhattan. The way he carried himself, you'd think Bumpy was the head of the New York Stock Exchange, heading down to Wall Street for the opening bell. In actuality, he probably had more power than anyone on Wall Street. He didn't just predict how businesses would perform. He actively determined how and *if* they would perform.

If you wanted to do business in Harlem, you went through Bumpy. And you paid him a percentage of your profits for the benefits of being in business in the neighborhood. It was like property tax—and hazard insurance. If you didn't want your hardware store, beauty salon, or grocery to go up in flames in the dead of night, you collected your fee every month and passed it off to one of Bumpy's associates.

But in the early days, I didn't see money change hands. Seemed to me like Bumpy made his living by reading the newspaper and going out to eat. Oh, and gambling. Bumpy spent a lot of time at the racetrack. Some afternoons, we'd stop at the track after lunch and I'd stay nearby and watch as Bumpy bet on the races. Then we might drive down to one of his favorite gambling spots so he could play a game of Skin, a card game similar to poker. From there, we might go to Frank's for dinner, and then I'd drive him home around eight. And that was it. No nightlife. He went to bed early. He might take his wife out to dinner or to a show every once in a while but that was rare. And even then he was home early.

"Let me tell you something," he said to me one night as we climbed the front steps of his brownstone.

"Yessir."

"You leave that life out there," he said, motioning to the street. "You cross the threshold of your home and that's it. Don't bring any of that into your home. Ever."

"Yessir."

"Dust yourself off and leave the trash outside. Be the king of your castle."

"Yessir."

For six months, I sat next to Bumpy, watching and observing. I saw a variety of celebrities come into his brownstone to visit. I saw the actor Sidney Poitier in the sitting room one afternoon, talking with Bumpy. On other occasions, I saw people like Billy Daniels and Billy Eckstine in the formal dining room for dinner. Of course, I never had conversations with these people. That wasn't my place. I just observed. And made sure to stay out of the way.

Occasionally, he'd give me tiny tasks. I'd be sent to see Fat Tony, out on Pleasant Avenue in East Harlem, to pick up a parcel and bring it back to him. I was never told what was in the packages and I never dared to ask. I wasn't even curious. It could've been a key of coke or an atom bomb. Didn't matter. I had tunnel vision when it came to his orders and never thought beyond completing the task exactly as he'd specified.

I did start to recognize certain faces as I observed his operations. At Frank's he often ate with Frank Molten, as I sat at a nearby table. Frank Molten was big time in Harlem.

I had no idea what business he was in but I saw him and Bumpy putting their heads together and talking in hushed tones often. Frank was a big guy but very elegant, looked like a real gentleman.

I knew I'd read something about Molten being involved in the drug trade somehow but I wasn't sure. And it wasn't my business so I didn't think about it for more than a half second.

I should say here that years later, I'd hear about how Bumpy Johnson was supposedly a big time drug dealer. I put my life on this statement right here: I didn't know nothing about Bumpy and drugs. He never whispered a word to me about it and I was with him from first thing in the morning till late at night. I'm not saying he wasn't. I'm just saying that if he was, he did it all without me hearing a word about it. I knew he took money from businesses, shook 'em down. A while after I started working for him, he had me going around to his businesses to collect. So that's what I knew. And that was all I knew. To this day, I don't know what else Bumpy was into.

Bumpy was paying me a little salary in those early days, about a hundred dollars a week. It was enough for me to get a little place of my own. After I moved out of his house, I would still be there first thing in the morning to start the day with him.

One of the servants would let me into the house and I'd wait in the front parlor for Bumpy to finish up his morning routine. A few mornings, I would see Miss Mayme, Bumpy's wife, as she gave orders to her employees and did her woman-of-the-house responsibilities.

Mayme Johnson was a good woman. Carried herself like

she was the First Lady of Harlem, which she was. She was always dressed up, but not too over the top. She carried herself like Jackie Kennedy would years later: stylish, refined, and soft-spoken.

"How are you doing this morning, Frank?" she would ask occasionally.

I'd remove my hat and nod a bit. "Morning, Miss Mayme," I'd say.

Now, we didn't talk much, maybe exchange some pleasantries about the weather. But not much more. I worked for Bumpy Johnson, not his wife. So I kept my conversation to the bare minimum.

I liked Mayme Johnson. She just passed away not too long ago. And I heard she'd been downing me in the press before she died. She wrote a book about her life with Bumpy and said I was nothing but Bumpy's flunky. Now, Mayme Johnson ain't a lying woman. And you better not call her a liar in my presence. Whatever she says is the way she remembers it. And I accept that.

But I do have to say this: Bumpy Johnson's wife didn't know anything about what her husband did for a living. I was with the man every day and barely knew all that he was into. He was always reminding me that work stayed far away from home, and he truly lived that. So I know Mayme Johnson didn't know much about what her husband did outside their home. But again, whatever she has said about me, I'll take it.

By the time a year had passed since our first meeting, I was officially Bumpy's right-hand man. I had bought a car, a Cadillac. (I wanted to buy a second car, but I knew Bumpy wouldn't approve. He wouldn't like the idea of his associate living a splashy lifestyle with two Cadillacs. So, I had to make do with just one.) I'd drive over to the brownstone on Mount Morris Park, park my car, and then go into the house, announce myself, get the keys to Bumpy's car, and wait outside for him to start his day.

"Dinner at Well's today, Luke," said Bumpy on one spring afternoon in the early 1950s.

"Yessir," I said, pulling off.

At Well's, I sat a few booths away from Bumpy. Bumpy didn't have to say a word to the waitstaff. The young woman brought over his usual order and a small cup of orange juice. I watched in silence as a few men came over to speak with him briefly.

The chimes at the door rattled and in came a tall, lanky young man with a shock of red hair styled in a straightened conk. He made his way to Bumpy's table and then stopped, waiting for permission from Bumpy before sitting down.

Bumpy smiled, just barely, and tilted his head to the side in a gesture that meant "have a seat."

The young man gave Bumpy a wide grin and then sat down at the table across from him, signaling for coffee from the waitress.

The two of them spoke briefly. I wasn't close enough to hear anything but I could tell it was a friendly, personal conversation. They didn't look like they were in any kind of business together.

The guy took one sip of his coffee, looked at his watch, and stood up.

"Gotta go. Good to see you, Mr. Johnson."

"Always good to see you. Careful out there, Red," said Bumpy, nodding his head before going back to his newspaper.

Just like all of Bumpy's associates, the guy he called Detroit Red didn't speak to me. I just watched him as he walked
out of the restaurant. He probably didn't even know my name
or know that I worked for Bumpy. But I knew him. I knew
they called him Detroit Red and I always recognized that
bright red hair he had. Years and years later, he would become Malcolm X. And even though he'd shaved off that conk
and cleaned up real good, the first time I saw him on the
news, I knew that he was the same Detroit Red who'd come
into Well's and have dinner with Bumpy sometimes.

Another frequent spot was an all-night diner on Fifty-
seventh Street and Seventh Avenue. Can't think of the name
of it to save my life. But I knew some mornings I'd have to
be ready at five thirty to get Bumpy to midtown by six. He'd
go straight to the back of the restaurant, and a few minutes
later, a man I'll call Fred Molino would come in with two of
his associates and head straight to the back as well.

I'd sit close enough to keep an eye on Bumpy but far
enough away that I couldn't hear anything. The waitresses
in that restaurant knew more about what Bumpy did for a
living than I did. I couldn't hear a thing they talked about. I
just knew they met for breakfast every so often and had
what looked like very serious, solemn discussions.

It was the equivalent of going to college. I was in school—
majoring in the underworld. I knew how to tell a gambling
addict from a drug addict. I could size up a man and tell if he
was a numbers runner or a pimp before he opened his
mouth. I could see what kind of women were tricking for
the hell of it.

I was now Bumpy's driver, bodyguard, and whatever else
he needed me to be. Wherever he went, to the pool hall, the

gambling spot, or the racetrack, I knew I was there to watch his back. And by doing so much observing, I learned to size up people pretty well and figure out their stories.

One morning, Bumpy slid into the backseat of the car and opened up one of his newspapers.

"Luke, you ever been on a plane?"

"No, sir," I said, my eyes on the red light in front of me.

"Never?"

"No, sir."

"Do you have a passport?"

"No, sir."

"You need to get one. Today. I'll make the arrangements. Do you have any identification? Birth certificate, anything like that?"

"No, sir."

"Don't worry about it. I'll take care of all of that."

"Yes, sir."

Bumpy flicked his newspaper open and it made a snapping sound.

"We're going to Cuba in the morning."

6

I couldn't have been more than eighteen years old. And I was sitting on an airplane for the first time in my life. A pretty, blond stewardess with a blinding white smile came to me and offered me a drink.

"No thank you, ma'am," I said. I was working. I knew better than to drink while I was on the job with Bumpy Johnson.

"Mr. Lucas," she said, leaning over so far that I could see every drop of her cleavage, "we're going to need you to fill out this paperwork before we land."

"Not a problem," I said. The slip of paper would explain who I was to Cuban authorities and, more important, why I was traveling there.

Name: FRANK LUCAS
Date of birth: September 9, 1930

Place of birth: La Grange, North Carolina
Occupation: _____

I stopped right there, my pencil in midair. Occupation? They didn't have enough room in that tiny space for me to write out what I did for Bumpy Johnson. I wondered what Bumpy put down as his occupation. He owned several legitimate businesses. And the few times I'd read about him in the paper, he was listed as the owner of an exterminating business. So he probably put that down. But me? I didn't have a job that could neatly fit on any form.

Occupation: driver/bodyguard/package picker-upper/confidant. That wouldn't work.

I thought about a movie I'd seen before the trip. The main character fantasized about the occupation he wished he had when it was time to fill out that line.

I picked my pencil back up and moved the paper in front of me on the tray.

Occupation: Actor

As soon as we landed, someone met us and led us to a waiting taxi. Before we got in to go to our hotel, the driver opened the trunk of the cab and handed me two .45s. I tucked them both into my waistband, where they would stay for the remainder of my trip.

I don't remember much about Cuba. I just know that Bumpy was in town to meet with a very well-known gangster I'm going to call Larry Lucci. I didn't know much about Lucci back then. I just knew I ended up sitting near both of them at several restaurants and private homes all around

Havana. I was strapped, with those .45s in my waistband. Bumpy seemed perfectly safe on this trip. And for important meetings in New York, he would have several people positioned at his meeting places. So this trip to Cuba must have been a low-pressure event.

I was always close enough to know if Bumpy was in any danger. But, just like in Harlem, I was never close enough to hear any conversations. It wasn't a tense trip. From what I remember, there was nothing but easy smiles and a relaxed atmosphere. I couldn't tell you if my life depended on it what Bumpy was there for.

Three days later, we were back in New York and back to business as usual. Breakfast at Frank's or the all-night diner, a trip to the racetrack, a few meetings over a few meals. And dropping Bumpy off at home while the night was still young.

But while Bumpy was at home reading and listening to classical music by nine, I was hitting the streets for the second part of my day. I had my wardrobe back together, a clean Cadillac, and a sweet bachelor's pad. So, I was able to turn my attention back to my own hobbies—drinking and carousing, hanging out in pool bars, and messing with the finest women in Harlem.

A year or two after our trip to Cuba, I picked up Bumpy for what I thought would be the usual schedule.

"Go to One Hundred Forty-sixth and Eighth Avenue, Luke."

"Yessir."

I parked the car right on the corner of 146th Street and 8th Avenue. There were two small corner stores with people streaming in and out. There was also a tiny storefront that I knew was one of Bumpy's numbers-running spots.

"Do you have any idea how much money flows in and out of Harlem in this unofficial lottery system?" Bumpy asked.

"No, sir, I don't."

"Millions. See that woman right there?" he said, pointing to an elderly woman wearing a janitor's jumpsuit.

"She hit for a hundred fifty thousand last year. She's putting two daughters and a niece through college. Gave twenty thousand to her church for a new rectory. Didn't even quit her job. And still playing a dollar every day. A dollar isn't a lot of money, is it, Luke?"

"No," I said. "It's not."

"And then there's men like that one," he said, pointing with his chin at a man in a suit, with a newspaper tucked under his arm.

"He looks like he's hot shit. He's going downtown to clean someone's office—in a suit! Can't afford to play more than a quarter a day. But he plays it. He'd skip lunch before he missed playing his number."

I just nodded my head.

"These people have to be treated with respect," Bumpy said. "This is a sensitive operation. It's illegal—God only knows why—so you have to watch out for the police. Avoid the good cops. Pay off the crooked ones. You have to have people working for you who are trustworthy and smart. I mean real smart." Bumpy tapped the side of his head for emphasis. "People who can keep track of hundreds of combinations, remember who owes what. Who's owed what. You hear me, Frank?"

"Yessir."

"Spot like this one? Right next to the subway line. Bring in at least a hundred grand a week."

I nodded.

"It's your responsibility now."

"Excuse me?" I asked.

"I'm assigning this spot to you. Already got a few folks doing all the running, collecting money and such. You need to make sure everything runs smoothly. Can you handle that?"

"Absolutely."

"Let me know if you have any problems," he said.

"I will."

"Though I expect you to handle this on your own. If you come to me, I'll assume you've already tried to handle it yourself."

"Yes, sir."

"You have to be honest, Luke," Bumpy said. "All you have is your word. In my business, you can't be dishonest. Gotta be straight up. You have to tell the truth. If it's something you can't say, just evade the question. Once you answer, you hit. Can't go there. Only speak the truth. You got that?"

"Yes, sir."

I threw myself into my new job, but I can't say I really liked it. Nothing but people coming in and out of that little storefront all day long, playing bets for pocket change, down to penny bets. And there were a few people, mostly pimps and hustlers, who would put down a hundred dollars. The odds were six to one. If you put down a dollar and your number hit, you'd come by the spot the next morning and pick up six dollars.

I had a staff: Lenny, Cornbread, One-Shot, and Cockeye. They collected the numbers, paid out the money, and kept a lookout for the police.

I was doing okay with money. I think Bumpy was now paying me about two hundred fifty dollars a week, which was a lot of money back then. Plus, I got a percentage of the profits from the numbers spot. I moved into a two-bedroom apartment at 66 St. Nicholas Place. This spot was even nicer than the place overlooking Central Park I'd had years before. St. Nicholas Place was the Park Avenue of Harlem. My building was about eight stories and had uniformed doormen on duty twenty-four hours a day. There were a lot of big-time people living in that area. I remember looking out my living-room window and seeing none other than Willie Mays playing stickball with the kids out there. He lived across the street in a different swanky building.

I remember one night, I was out socializing at the Theresa Hotel on 125th and 7th Avenue and Bumpy came into the nightclub. It was rare for him to hang out and I was surprised to see him there. He was in a corner of the club, just as quiet as usual, listening to the jazz band. He had his eyes closed, oblivious to all the debauchery going on in the rest of the club.

I had my eye on this fine-ass Chinese woman. She was at the bar, I was at a table nearby. Every time I caught her eye, she smiled, and I wanted to melt. She was just that fine. I sidled up next to her, giving her my best sweet talk.

"I think that gentleman is trying to get your attention," she said, pointing to the back of the bar.

I looked and saw Bumpy beckoning to me.

"I'll be right back."

"Do you know who you're talking to?" Bumpy said.

"Should I know?"

"Yes, Frank, you should."

I looked at the woman again. There was nothing unusual about her at all, at least not to me. You didn't see Asian women too often up in Harlem. But I'd seen a few. None as fine as that one there.

"You should know she's spoken for," he said. He nodded toward the door.

None other than Joe Louis came through the door just then and went right over to the woman and kissed her. Joe Louis! Now, I was a badass at this time in my life. But even I couldn't deny that seeing Joe Louis was a big deal.

Joe made the rounds around the club and then headed back to pay his respects to Bumpy.

"Always good to see you, Mr. Johnson," he said, removing his hat.

"Joe, this is Frank Lucas, he works with me."

Joe pumped my hand and smiled. "Good to meet you, Frank."

Joe was one of those people you just liked right away. Of course, as a black man, I'd followed his career with great pride, especially when he beat Max Schmelling. But besides that, he was just an all-around good guy. I'd heard that he donated his entire purse to the war effort after several fights. How could you not like a guy who would do that? I ended up becoming friendly with Joe. When he was in town, we might have a drink together or just hang out at a club for a minute. I wasn't big on having a whole lot of personal friends. But Joe Louis quickly became one of the few.

I liked working for Bumpy. But to tell the truth, managing the numbers spot bored the shit out of me. It was pure drudgery. All of these small-minded people making their tiny little bets day after day after day. And all the big money going to—going to where? I sure didn't know.

And I was still collecting money for Bumpy, too. I collected more than a million a month from different businesses for protection. And I wasn't the only person collecting for him, so I can't imagine how much he was making.

I didn't mind going from store to store collecting the money. But I hated counting it. Every once in a while I'd bring a briefcase or a valise or a plain shopping bag full of money to Bumpy and he'd glance over it and say, "Count that out for me, Luke."

Ain't that I can't count. It's just a dirty, tedious job. You might lose your place and gotta start all over. Drove me crazy. Especially when it wasn't my money.

Some nights, I'd lean against the hood of my Cadillac, talking to some pretty young thing who stopped to say hello. And half of me would be telling her whatever she needed to hear to get her ass into my bed that night. But the other half of me would be daydreaming. Did I come to Harlem for this? To be comfortable? To have an apartment and a car and a regular job? I was in the underworld and always ran a risk of getting locked up for being involved in the numbers, and the payoff just didn't seem worth it. What did I have to do to make it big? If I was going to wake up every day knowing that I could get arrested and go to jail, shouldn't I be going hard to make some serious money?

Nearly a year went by as I wondered what my future would hold. In the meantime, I continued collecting for Bumpy. And I managed my numbers spot with no problems. Until a group of corrections officers who always played the same combination came into my spot, claiming they'd hit.

"You know we always play six four two," said Bobby Jackson, the guy who usually played the number for the group of officers.

"I know what number y'all *usually* play," I said. "But you didn't play it yesterday."

I didn't look up from my slips. I'd checked, double-checked, and tripled-checked. There was no slip from them. It was common for people to forget to play, and then if their number came out, they'd try to get away with having the runner believe they'd played the number. Didn't work with me. Jackson hadn't played. Plain and simple.

"This is some bullshit. You owe us three thousand dollars," Jackson said.

"I don't owe you shit but a kick in the ass if you don't get the fuck out of here."

I went to Bumpy to let him know what was going on.

"I told you when I put you over there," he said. "You have to handle it yourself. I'm sure you can do it."

The next day, Jackson came back, with three of the officers who always played that number together. And they were all in uniform, with weapons in their waistbands.

"I want to get paid now, Frank," Jackson said.

"Not a single dime," I said.

Jackson whipped out his gun and fired off a shot in my direction. I dived behind the counter in the store and grabbed my own gun. There was nowhere for me to run because I was trapped in the back of the store. I was going to have to shoot or be shot. I came up just a bit, pointed my gun, and shot it. As soon as they saw my gun, they ran out of the store, still shooting at me.

It was broad daylight and I chased them right out of the

numbers spot, still shooting. The people on the street started screaming and diving for cover. All the while, I'm still chasing these fools down the street, shooting at them and ducking their bullets at the same time.

It was a bad scene. But once they started shooting at me in the store, I had no choice but to return the favor. Innocent people could have been killed and I didn't think about any of that at the time. I wanted those officers dead.

The officers all ran onto a bus and started making their way to the back of it. I had the audacity to start shooting directly into the bus, shattering all the windows, while the people on the bus screamed in terror. The officers ducked, and a few of them shot back. I ran down the street, alongside the bus. I shot out every window on the side of the bus I could see.

When I heard the sirens of a police car on the way, I snapped out of the rage and hauled ass out of the area. I wasn't worried about people telling the cops about me. By that time, everyone knew I worked for Bumpy Johnson. They wouldn't say a word, if they knew what was good for them.

I even went back to the scene of the crime an hour or so later. The cops were there, trying to get the scene cleaned up and asking people questions.

"Excuse me," said a white man with a notebook in his hand.

I just raised an eyebrow to acknowledge him without speaking.

"Walter Winchell," he said, thrusting out his hand. I shook it without saying a word. I knew exactly who Walter Winchell was. He was the most popular news columnist in the country. He knew stuff happened as it was happening.

"Looks like you're in a bit of trouble," Winchell said. He flipped his notebook to a fresh sheet and licked the tip of his pencil.

"I have no idea what you are talking about," I said.

"Sure you do. Don't you work with Bumpy Johnson? I know this is his territory. Which means you probably work for him."

"Bumpy who?" I said.

Winchell smiled. "I guess you have no comment."

I smiled back. "Nice to meet you Mr. Winchell."

He held out a business card. "If you ever want to talk. You know, about anything, here's where you can reach me."

I nodded.

"And I guess if I need to reach you . . ." he said.

"I don't see that ever being necessary," I said, walking away.

But Winchell would continually find me over the years. I'd never give him any quotes. But we'd talk regularly. That's how a good reporter gets his goods, keeping an ear to the streets. And he definitely made sure to check in with me just to say hello.

The next close call I had came when Bumpy had a confrontation with some people who owed him money. Bumpy didn't just shake down businesses in Harlem. If anyone made any money doing anything illegal, Bumpy was owed a piece of that, too. Soon after I started working for him, some guys from Harlem pulled a job off out in the Midwest, robbed some diamonds from somewhere. And they sent Bumpy his share of the heist. That kind of thing happened quite often.

One time, Bumpy was expecting his share of jewels from

a robbery, but instead, he was sent fake gems. He came up to the numbers hole where I was working to see me.

"You got your piece?" he asked, as soon as he walked inside.

"Yessir," I said.

"Let's go."

We got into his Lincoln and sped down the East River Drive to a jewelry store on Canal Street.

"Where is he?" Bumpy asked.

An elderly white man looked up, alarmed. "Mr. Johnson, no one is here but me, I swear to you!"

Bumpy pointed to a back door and I tried to open it. It was locked.

"Open it, Luke," he said.

I kicked the door down. There were six older white men standing there.

"Where are my fucking diamonds?" Bumpy said to one guy.

"This ain't how we're doing this, Bumpy," the guy said.

I just watched the other men. We were outnumbered. But it didn't matter. If they made a single twitchy move, I'd shoot them all dead.

"You want me to show you how we're doing this?" Bumpy asked. He pulled his hand back and smacked the shit out of that man. None of his people moved a muscle. He motioned for Bumpy to join him in a back room. I kept my eyes on the five people left in the office and they kept their eyes on me. I don't know what took place back there but when Bumpy came out, he was satisfied.

"Let's go, Luke," he said.

I faithfully followed Bumpy's direction that day and every

other day. I told the truth and kept my word. If I couldn't do either, I kept my eyes open.

A few years after I started working with Bumpy, Icepick Red was still running the streets, killing people for money, and generally being a menace to society. I know Bumpy kept tabs on everything he did. He knew what everyone in Harlem did. But finally, Icepick had gone too far and Bumpy had to make an example out of him.

There was a guy named Little Willie who worked for Bumpy. Like a lot of men in the street life, he had a fancy house out in Englewood Cliffs for his wife and children. I knew he had a daughter about eight or nine years old and a son who was just a little baby. Well, for some reason, Icepick Red decided he was going to rob Little Willie. To this day, I can't figure out why that man would do something like that. Robbing one of Bumpy's men was suicide, plain and simple.

On one cold, wintry night, I had just dropped Bumpy off at home. I was waiting around to make sure he didn't need me for anything else when I saw him take a phone call. Suddenly, a worried expression came across his face and he just stared at the wall in his living room.

I could tell by the look on his face that whatever news he was getting on the other end of that phone was not good at all.

"Luke, get your boys," he said.

He stood up and put his coat back on and headed to the back of the house. I made a call and then went outside to wait for my crew to show up. Within minutes, Cockeye, Shoestring, Little Bit, and Doc Holliday were pulling up, waiting to get their instructions.

Bumpy came out to my car and got inside.

"We're going to Englewood Cliffs," he said. His lips set in a tight line. "Icepick robbed Little Willie."

I could hear bloodcurdling screams as soon as we pulled onto the street in New Jersey. I wasn't sure what was going on but the screaming was loud and intense.

We all went into the house and saw a horrible scene. Little Willie was dead, sprawled out on the living-room floor of his fancy house. There was blood pooled underneath him and an ice pick sticking straight out of his chest. Willie's wife was naked, huddling on the floor near the stairs, screaming and crying.

Bumpy immediately went to Willie's wife and put his overcoat across her shoulders. He kept asking her what had happened but she just kept screaming and screaming. Their little girl, not more than eight years old, was at the top of the stairs. She looked like she was in shock.

"What happened?" Bumpy asked one more time.

"Willie told him where the money was," the wife said. "And Icepick took the money. But he still tied Willie up! And then . . . and then he raped me."

The wife started bawling again. And everyone in the room dropped their heads and looked away.

"Right in front of him, Bumpy," the wife said. "He attacked me right in front of Willie and my kids. And then he killed him!"

The wife dissolved into more tears and Bumpy tried to comfort her.

"Luke, you stay here," Bumpy said. "The rest of you all. Go."

Bumpy and I got the wife together, called some of her

relatives, and then we took her to the Theresa Hotel. I waited in the car while Bumpy got her all checked in and waited for the family to come and take care of her and the children. Bumpy came back to the car and exhaled as he sat back.

"She's on the top floor, Luke," he said. "If you hear from her, take her whatever she needs."

"Yes, sir," I said.

I drove Bumpy back to the house in Mount Morris Park. He got out and stood in front of the car before going inside.

"Go get Icepick Red. I want to see him. Immediately."

"Yessir."

The next night, me and Doc Holliday saw Icepick Red leaning up against a lamppost on the corner of 134th Street and 7th Avenue. It was dusk and it was rainy. I wasn't sure it was really him. But as we walked up the street, Doc touched my side with his elbow and jutted his chin in the direction of the tall, lanky man standing there.

I stopped a few feet away from Icepick. Doc kept walking until he was right next to him.

"Let's go, Red," I said. "Boss wants to see you."

Icepick looked me up and down, brought up a noisy batch of phlegm, and spit on the sidewalk right in between us.

"I ain't got no time for that bullshit," Icepick Red said.

I thought about the scene the night before at Little Willie's house, the little girl wandering around in a daze, the baby crying, Little Willie on the floor with the ice pick in his chest, and his wife naked and screaming. Icepick was crazy. I knew Bumpy was going to punish him. And I knew he had to know that Bumpy was going to punish him. Why would he do it?

I couldn't imagine. And it wasn't my job to figure it out. It was my job to bring him to Bumpy.

"Let's go, Red," I said again.

"Ain't going nowhere."

With no hesitation, I pulled out my .44 and cocked it. With a loud snap, my gun was in position. Icepick jumped. I'd pulled it out so fast, he hadn't even had a chance to reach for his own weapon. And with Doc standing less than a foot away, he knew he wasn't getting away.

"Stop popping all that shit and let's go," I said.

We took him back to the car, where Chickenfoot was waiting in the backseat. I got in the driver's seat while Doc and Chickenfoot sat on either side of Icepick Red, with Doc jabbing a handgun into Red's side. If he moved a muscle, Doc would have shot him dead. If I had known what Bumpy had planned for Icepick Red, I would have just told Doc to shoot him right there.

Back at Mount Morris, I let Bumpy know we had Icepick. He came outside immediately, dressed smartly as always, in a topcoat and hat, wearing leather gloves to shield his hands from the cold night air.

"Luke, come get in the car with me."

"Yes, sir."

Bumpy got into the car and I told the guys to follow us in my car. Bumpy directed me to a mammoth abandoned apartment building over on the southwest corner of 141st Street and 7th Avenue. Bumpy had the crew take Red downstairs to the basement, strip him naked, and cuff him to the large pipes.

I watched Bumpy take two small jars and a paintbrush out of the inside pocket of his topcoat. One looked like syrup or honey. The other had something moving around inside but I couldn't make out what it was. He stuffed his handkerchief into Icepick's mouth and used duct tape to shut it. Icepick was on the ground, his eyes wild, moving and squirming, not knowing what was coming next. None of us knew.

"Some people are just animals," Bumpy said softly. "Not worthy of life."

He took out a small knife and cut deeply across Icepick's face, on both sides of his eyelids and across his neck. If he hadn't had his mouth stuffed with the handkerchief, we might have heard his screams. But they were just low and muffled.

Bumpy calmly opened one jar, poured the sticky substance onto the brush and rubbed it into Icepick's eyes. Then he dipped the brush into the jar again and rubbed it over Icepick's privates. He picked up the second jar and held it up. Now I could see what was in there: hundreds of fire ants. I felt my stomach flip over as I watched Bumpy open the jar and dump the ants all over Icepick's eyes and privates. Somehow, he was able to start screaming and I could hear him yelling even through the handkerchief stuffed in his mouth.

I couldn't even imagine where Bumpy had gotten fire ants. I grew up seeing them in the South. But I knew you wouldn't see them in Harlem. Bumpy always had a way of getting his hands on anything he wanted or needed.

I had to look away. Because that scene was almost worse than what I'd seen the night before at Little Willie's house.

"Let's go," Bumpy said.

We all filed out of the basement silently. The only thing I could hear were the tortured, muffled screams of Icepick

Red. I can still hear them in my head today, as a matter of fact.

Bumpy told me to drive him back there the next day. Icepick Red was still alive. And completely out of his mind.

Bumpy dumped more ants onto Icepick Red and spit on him, just the way Icepick always spit everywhere.

"Why don't you just shoot him?" I asked Bumpy.

"He doesn't deserve to die that easy," Bumpy said.

We left the building once more. And left Icepick to die. I went back a few days later to make sure he was dead. And of course, he was. What I saw remaining was—literally—just a shell of a human. Never seen anything like it before or since.

I have to admit, I left that basement with tears in my eyes. And this is Icepick Red we're talking about. He was a stone-cold killer. But still, what I saw in that basement really messed me up. Don't get me wrong. Icepick definitely had to die. But not like that. When I got back into the car to leave, I found myself wishing that I'd just shot him dead as he leaned up against that lamppost that night.

I knew why Bumpy had reacted so strongly. He'd had no choice. He was the biggest thing in New York City. And any man who worked for him was hands-off. He could not let anyone think that they could do what Icepick Red had done to Little Willie and his family and get away with it. And he couldn't just kill him. He had to make an example out of him. After Icepick's body was discovered, the streets were buzzing for weeks. People knew what Bumpy was capable of. And nothing like what happened to Little Willie would ever happen again.

That situation also let me know exactly what I was dealing with. Bumpy was my boss. And he was the boss of all bosses. I knew two things. I knew that he would do the same thing for me if anyone ever disrespected me.

I also knew that he would do the same thing *to* me if he ever felt like it was necessary. They were two lessons I hoped I never needed to learn firsthand.

7

I would soon learn that all the ugliness I saw in the world was often tempered by beautiful things. There would be a few times when I would have to shift gears from seeing pure horror, like what had happened to Icepick Red, to beautiful things like the birth of a new child.

On one spring afternoon in May 1960, I had to shut everything down for a minute to soak in the wonder of a new life that I had brought into the world.

"Look at this baby," I said, half to myself. "A little Frank Lucas."

I held my newborn son in my arms and watched him open his eyes and look at me with interest.

"You gotta do the right thing, little Frank," I whispered to my firstborn son. "Get an education. And don't be no junkie."

I had met a woman named Jonita in the late 1950s. She was from Harlem. When I first met her, she was dating some guy named Eddie who hated my guts. Don't know why. But he couldn't stand me. I liked Jonita. She was about five feet five inches tall, brown skinned, with a nice petite shape and a good head of hair. I didn't give any thought to her man Eddie when we started messing around. He was her business. Not mine. I actually ended up fighting Eddie over a game of craps soon after I'd started seeing Jonita. I think he saw me and Jonita together a time or two and that's what the fight was really about. I didn't care one way or another.

I liked Jonita fine, but I wasn't looking for a wife. Jonita joined a long list of women in my life. And it seemed like all I had to do was look at a woman and she'd be knocked up with my baby.

Jonita had three other children, all boys, and they all lived together in Harlem.

It wasn't long after we'd been messing around that Jonita told me she was pregnant. I already had my twin daughters down in North Carolina, so I remember hoping that this new child would be a boy. And sure enough, I went up to Metropolitan Hospital after I got word that she'd had the baby, and I stood at the window in her room and held my son, whom I named Frank, in my arms for the first time.

Jonita and her boys, including my son, were all set up in Harlem and I came through to pick up my son whenever I could. He was born in the spring. And by the fall of 1960, I was in a situation that would make it much harder for me to go see him.

I got arrested for conspiracy to sell drugs and sentenced to thirty months in the federal penitentiary in Lewisburg, out on Route 80 in central Pennsylvania. Jonita brought my son to see me every weekend, which I appreciated. Doing jail time was no big deal to me. But what made it a little complicated was that they had blacks and whites desegregated. Around the time I went into Lewisburg, they'd passed some law that made it illegal to segregate prisoners. So, for the first time, in the common areas and in the mess hall, black folks and white folks were together. I'm not so sure that was a good idea back then 'cause, for the most part, blacks and whites in jail were like the Bloods and Crips today.

And at Lewisburg, there were more white boys. We were outnumbered at least three to one, which just added to the tension when they started mixing us up. My plan was to keep my nose clean for thirty months and get out and get back to hustling and working for Bumpy. I wasn't trying to get mixed up in any racial bullshit. But at the same time, I do have a severe temper and I never let anyone, black or white, disrespect me without paying the price for it.

I had mess-hall duty in Lewisburg. One of my responsibilities was distributing coffee to the inmates at mealtime. We weren't allowed to go up and pour ourselves a cup of coffee. So my job was to wheel around these huge drums of coffee to each table and pour a cup for each inmate. There was this one inmate, don't remember his name. Only remember he looked just like Mr. Clean, same shaved head, same big-ass muscles. His arms were as big as an average man's legs. Couldn't stand him. Always bossing people around, talking shit, and acting like a jerk.

"You gon' bring some coffee to my table or not, mother-fucker," he said one afternoon at lunch.

"Ain't get over that way yet," I said, trying hard not to say anything else.

"Well, you better get over here quick before I stomp the hell out of you."

His little crew laughed and I could feel my blood start simmering.

"Still ain't moving fast enough, boy," he said. "Bring my coffee now. Them boys you serving can wait."

I looked down at the black men sitting at the table I was serving right then. They were all men I was pretty friendly with and they had a look in their eyes I will never forget. They were pissed off and full of rage, just like I was. We were all criminals. But that didn't mean those white boys had any right whatsoever to act like they were the wardens. I worked in the mess hall. I didn't work for him or any of his friends.

And the worst part about it all? That motherfucker really thought I was scared of him! He sneered at me and had this look in his eyes that was outright daring me to challenge the way he was talking.

Now, starting some trouble could mean no visitation. And I looked forward to Jonita bringing my son to see me on the weekends. But I damn sure wasn't going to let Mr. Clean think he was the boss of me.

I rolled the five-gallon container of coffee over to where Mr. Clean sat.

"You ready for your coffee?" I asked.

"You goddamn right, boy," he said, holding out his cup and laughing. He didn't even turn around to look at me. Just held his cup in the air while he was looking at his friends.

I overturned that whole container on that white boy's head and soaked him with scalding coffee from his head to his nuts. It's pretty damn nasty, what some hot coffee can do to your skin. His face immediately turned even whiter and then blisters began to form.

That man was screaming like a two-dollar whore. And

then here come some of his buddies from the table, ready to lay me out on the floor. I was so enraged that I felt like I had superhuman strength. I truly believe that I would have been able to take on every single one of them. But I didn't have to. My boys were on their feet as soon as I dumped that coffee; they had forks and homemade shanks and anything else they could fashion as a weapon. Every black man in that joint had my back. We tore that room up, giving them white folks just what they deserved. We fought for I don't know how long before I found myself in a choke hold.

"That's it!" someone said, his hands on my shoulder. "It's over now, Lucas."

I didn't know who was putting his hands on me. I just reacted and socked him right in the jaw. It wasn't until I got jumped by all the guards that I realized I had punched out a prison lieutenant. They beat the shit out of me. And then I was thrown into the hole for two or three days.

But, interestingly, I didn't get charged with anything. Everyone knew that white boy got exactly what was coming to him. I heard he was thoroughly fucked up. And spent a few days in the prison hospital. I was glad to hear that, too. He deserved every ounce of pain he felt.

I didn't always have problems with the white boys in prison. In fact, during that same prison sentence, I was in a dormitory with a few white boys I was actually pretty cool with. One of them was Vincent "The Chin" Gigante. For a while, I slept in a dormitory between him and another guy we called Herbie. For about two years, we shared the same area. Now, I knew what Vincent did for a living on the outside. He had a pretty high ranking in the Genovese crime family.

Vincent knew I worked for Bumpy Johnson, but we never

talked business. There was a mutual respect but there was also an understanding that we wouldn't talk about the street stuff on the inside. We wouldn't have had anything to talk about in that sense anyway. We talked mostly about sports. Vincent told me about how he loved boxing, and he was amazed that I was close personal friends with none other than Joe Louis. The Mets had just joined the National League, replacing the Brooklyn Dodgers. So, we talked baseball a lot, too.

"Who you got your money on this week?" Vincent might say to me on a Sunday night as we listened to the radio announcer talk about a game.

"The Mets are terrible," I'd say. "You know it and I know it."

"Eh, we'll see what happens."

"I know what I'm talking about, Gigante. You'll see."

We'd rib each other here and there about our teams and bullshit about topics in the news. I can't say we were friends. But I did respect him. From everything I observed, he was a stand-up guy, and we never had any problems.

I got out of Lewisburg after thirty months. My son was now walking and talking and he was always happy to see me. I got out and never gave one single thought to the straight life. I reported right back to Bumpy and waited for instruction on the next step and the next assignment. I settled back into the street life very easily. It was all I knew. And at the time, it was all I wanted to know.

8

At my place on St. Nicholas, I watched the evening news every night. As more and more troops were shipped to Vietnam, it became the number-one discussion on the news. One night, I heard the newscasters talking about a lot of the soldiers getting hooked on the heroin supplied out of the Golden Triangle, which included Burma, Laos, Thailand, and Vietnam. The reporter said the soldiers were getting hooked after their first time and that the heroin was cheaper and stronger than anything that could be found in the United States.

Cheaper and stronger. Cheaper and stronger. Cheaper and stronger.

Those words bounced around in my head for weeks, like a song that gets stuck in your mind and you can't stop singing the lyrics. I was no stranger to the drug trade. I'd already bought and sold a million dollars' worth of heroin before I'd even met Bumpy. And I remember the first batch I put out. My cousin Fletcher told me that he had nearly OD'd because I'd cut it too strong. And when I learned to cut it better, I made more money because my heroin lasted longer.

I started thinking about the chain of command in business. I worked for Bumpy, the boss of bosses. But even if he didn't have a boss, there were people he had to answer to on some level.

What if you could skip a step? What if you could jump right to the head of the line and make deals with the top tier? I thought about Old Man Pop, who had sold me my first batch of heroin. Where did Old Man Pop get his supply from? I knew he made a profit every time I bought from him. And I knew that Old Man Pop's supplier made a profit every time he bought. When did it stop?

Someone once told me that if you stand on the roof of a tall building and look down, you'll never see people look up. They're worker bees, scurrying here and there to get wherever they have to go. They don't have the time or the inclination to look up at the sky. But little kids will look up. Stand on a roof sometime and try it. If you look for a long time, you'll see all sorts of people walking back and forth. The only people who will ever look up and notice you there will be small children. They know that things happen everywhere—not just in front of you or behind you.

I knew everything that was behind me, my life in North Carolina, my poor cousin shot and killed for no goddamn reason, my trials and travails from North Carolina to Kentucky, and my journey to Harlem. My first earnings of all, lost playing craps and pool. My introduction to Bumpy Johnson. That was all behind me.

I saw what was in front of me: working for Bumpy, maybe managing more and more of his numbers spots. I could get killed by someone trying to take over Bumpy's territory. I could go to jail for anything.

So, instead of just looking forward and backward, I looked up.

And just like that, a random thought popped into my head, while I lay splayed out on my leather couch, the evening news still blaring in the background, my eyes on the ceiling.

What if I could go straight to the source and buy heroin from Southeast Asia and bring it back to Harlem?

Before I could even get the thought fully formed in my mind, I knew without a shadow of a doubt that I could do it. What would stop me? Fear? Hell no. I didn't have any. I made up my mind to talk it over with Bumpy the first chance I got. If he gave me the okay, I'd leave as soon as I could work out all the details. I figured he might be interested in expanding his empire. And at the same time, I'd be able to stop feeling like I was standing still in Harlem. I wanted to see the world and travel—and make a shitload of money at the same time.

If he could finance my plan, I'd make us both richer than he could imagine. I could fulfill my own dreams while extending Bumpy's power base throughout New York.

He'd have to go for it. No way he'd turn down a plan like that. No way at all.

One morning, I told Bumpy I needed to talk to him about something. He simply nodded his head, as always, and went back to his newspaper. Later that afternoon, as we drove off from lunch at Frank's, he finally spoke.

"You said you needed to talk to me, Luke," Bumpy said.

"Yes, sir."

"Pull over."

Of course, we couldn't talk about anything important in the car. Bumpy knew that at any time, it was most likely bugged by the FBI. So we never discussed anything important in the car. Always somewhere right out in the open. Bumpy also told me that most law-enforcement agencies had people who could read lips. So I picked up his habit of shielding my mouth with my hand when I spoke. To this day, if I'm talking about something important, I'll hold my hand up to my lips before I speak. Old habits die hard, I guess.

We stood outside the numbers hole I was managing.

"Been watching the news," I said. "Soldiers getting strung out quick and hard on that stuff out there."

Bumpy just nodded, his eyes on the street.

"I'm thinking of going over there. I'll come back with it. Everyone else has to get their stuff from the guineas. We can sell it ourselves without dealing with the guineas downtown."

Bumpy gestured for me to walk up the street. We walked quietly for about five minutes and then stopped in front of an apartment building.

"What are you saying, Luke?"

"I could do it. I know I could. Get the stuff straight from the Asians. Bring it back and sell it."

Bumpy seemed to be turning it over in his mind, but his face was expressionless.

"I don't know about that, Luke."

"I know I could do it."

"No, Frank," he said firmly. "We're not going to do that."

"We could keep it quiet. No one but me and you would ever have to even know that—"

"It ain't time for that, Frankie," he said. "Just ain't time."

By the look on Bumpy's face, I could tell that the conversation was finished. I was disappointed. But I dismissed it quickly. Bumpy knew a lot more than I did about how things were operating. And I figured he had a good reason for not wanting me to go to Southeast Asia. But for the life of me, I sure couldn't think of what it could be.

I knew better than to bring it up to Bumpy again. He had said no. And that was that. I slipped back into my routine, picking up his cash from various businesses, running my numbers spot, chasing women. But I was just going through the motions. Every once in a while I'd look up at the sky and wonder if I'd ever be able to take a shot at the big time.

9

It was around this time that I began to travel as much as I could. I had enough money in my pockets, and Bumpy had associates all over the world that would look out for me if I needed anything. I've always been the restless type. I can't stay in one place for too long without feeling antsy. After the trip to Cuba, I started taking small trips alone: a weekend in Puerto Rico, a long weekend in Vegas, hanging out at the craps table.

Eventually, I started traveling farther: Paris, Istanbul, Monaco. I can't remember the first international trip I took, but I do remember hearing that Monaco was heaven for gamblers. So I booked myself a flight, packed a small bag, and left.

Twenty-four hours later, I was standing outside the Monte Carlo Casino, in plain view of the route that the race-car drivers used for the Monte Carlo Grand Prix.

I could get used to this, I thought to myself.

I sampled a little French food, but spent most of my time gambling. I also met a few Frenchwomen who were more than a little bit friendly. It was a short trip but it definitely whetted my appetite for more travel. I can't even remember how many times I ended up going to Paris. But it became just as normal for me to go there for a weekend as it was for other people to go to a movie on a Saturday night.

The European cities began to blur together. I'd hop off my flight, ask around for the best hotel, take a taxi, have a meal, go to the casino, meet some women, and start over the next day before hopping on a flight back home.

Sometimes, my work associates wouldn't even know I'd gone anywhere at all. I learned to dip in and out of the country with ease. I loved the feeling of being somewhere thousands of miles from Harlem and then back in town before anyone could miss me. I'll bet there were people who would swear they saw me at my usual haunts when I was really halfway around the world.

Traveling opened my eyes to adventure. And I saw how much money there was to be made in the world. I wanted it—all of it. I knew I couldn't ask Bumpy again about my plans to sell heroin wholesale. But I couldn't stop thinking about my plan and why Bumpy didn't want to do it.

People have often asked me if Bumpy was in the drug game. If he was, I didn't know anything about it. I know he went to prison a few times while I worked for him. I asked no questions. And I didn't visit him—ever. When he was locked up, he didn't want people too close to him to visit. He was watched carefully in jail. They knew he was still running things from prison and he didn't want extra heat. I would get word from other associates on what he needed me to do to keep things running smoothly. And Bumpy's enterprises were such a well-oiled machine that nothing missed a beat when he was in prison. And when he got out, everything was right back in step.

The papers claimed he got arrested on narcotics charges. I can only say that *I* didn't know anything about Bumpy and the drug game. Put me on the stand and I will tell the jury: I didn't know anything about what Bumpy did. That's a fact. I moved packages for him and couldn't tell you what was in them. I'm sure Bumpy wanted things that way. I was close to him. But he kept certain things from me. And that was perfectly fine with me.

Bumpy didn't seem to have any interest in the drug game, at least to me. But I was interested—very interested. And I dabbled here and there with selling what I needed to keep my funds up. I still wanted to set up a global operation so I wouldn't have to depend on a middle man. But in the meantime, I had to do it any way I could.

I got caught here and there but never with any serious consequences. A week in jail here and there. Nothing much more serious. I wasn't worried about jail; if anything, I was more worried about not being available for Bumpy if he needed me for anything. I did the best I could to manage both jobs and I did it pretty well. I know Bumpy must have been aware that I was in the drug game, but he never said a word to me about it, and I didn't mention it, either. But I did know that nothing happened in Harlem that Bumpy didn't know about. When I first met him, he already knew about all the trouble I'd gotten into. And I was just a random, homeless street kid.

By the late 1960s, I was living in the River Bend Apartments on 5th Avenue and 139th Street. Pretty fancy place. I was married to a woman I'll call Miriam. I met Miriam at The Paradise, over on 110th Street and 8th Avenue. She was real tall, I remember that. And had a pair of legs that went on forever. We were dating pretty heavy although I always continued to do my own thing. She was always needling me to get married. I finally agreed—for no other reason than I wanted her off my back. I didn't take marriage vows very seriously. You want me to say I do? Sure. Until I don't anymore. Then I'm out of there. Over the years, women would think that was a big deal, getting me down to the altar. But it wasn't no big deal. I'd say "I do" if I cared about you a half a whit. Didn't mean I wouldn't walk away without looking back if you worked my nerves enough.

Miriam was alright by me. But I spent just as much time in hotels with other women as I did in the apartment with her. I can't say I didn't care about her because I did. But it just wasn't that big of a deal to me. I was moving in too many directions and I had seen too much violence in my life to get all caught up in feelings and emotions.

The morning that Miriam told me she was pregnant, my attitude changed a bit. I've never shied away from fatherhood. I believe children are a blessing. I already had three children at that point and I didn't mind having more.

"How far along are you?" I asked Miriam.

"Not sure," she said, curled up on the couch in the living room. "About six weeks."

"I told you all I gotta do is look at a woman and she'll be pregnant."

"Well, you did more than look at me."

"You right about that," I said.

Miriam looked down at the floor and then back up at me. "Once we have this baby, are you gonna do right by me?"

"What's that supposed to mean?"

"You know exactly what I mean, Frank Lucas. You're gone for weeks at a time. I hear about the women in the clubs that you take back to hotels. I don't like it."

"Don't tell me what you like and what you don't like."

"If we're gonna raise a family together, I would think you'd change up your behavior at least a little. It's disrespectful!"

I rolled my eyes and got up. "You knew what you were getting when you begged me to marry you. Don't try to change me up now." I walked out of the apartment, slamming the door behind me.

Women had always worked my nerves. I loved the chase. I love the first night of making love in a hotel room. I loved it all. But it seemed like as soon as I met a woman who was halfway decent, she started begging for something more. And it would never ever be enough. Very annoying.

That night, I drove out to The Dugout, a beautiful spot in Queens where black folks would get the white-tablecloth treatment from the owner, Marguerite Mays, the wife of the baseball player Willie Mays. The Dugout was a special place for me. I could take a date there and know that we would be treated right. Or I could go alone and just have a drink and watch the clientele. There were so many beautiful women in The Dugout, I rarely left that place alone at the end of the night.

That night, I sat at a table with bottle service and watched a beautiful creature talking to people at the bar. She truly

looked like she could have graced the cover of *Vogue*. She had
her legs crossed just enough for me to see that she had pretty
thighs and a beautiful ass. Cocoa-brown skin, a smile from
here to heaven, and a great physique. She was sitting there
talking to Walt Frazier, who had just started playing for the
Knicks. They looked like they were definitely a couple, but
that didn't matter to me. I knew Walt well. He was no competition whatsoever. I knew without a doubt that I was going to
have a bit of fun with her. As soon as Walt left her side for a
minute, I was right there to make my move.

"What's your name?"

"Billie."

I put my hand to her hair. "Billie, you don't have to
worry about anything else this evening."

"Is that so?"

"That is very so. I'm Frank Lucas. Have you eaten dinner?"

"Not yet. I'm about to have a bite with a friend."

"Yes, you are. Me."

"I don't even know you!"

I took Billie's hand and led her out of the restaurant with
confidence.

"Mr. Lucas, I don't usually have dinner with strange men."

"You know who I am. Don't act like you don't."

Billie just smiled. "Maybe I do. Maybe I don't."

"Get in the car," I said.

I held the door for Billie, closed it behind her, and then
got in on my side. I peeled off and got onto the highway.

"Where are we dining?" she asked.

"You'll see when we get there."

I took her home to pack a bag and then we drove to the

long-term parking lot at JFK Airport. I parked the car and went around and opened the door for her.

"We're eating at the airport?"

"Do you always ask so many damn questions? Close your mouth, girl!"

Billie made a big show out of pretending to lock her mouth with a key and throw it away. I told her to sit down in a lounge area while I made arrangements. I called Miriam and told her I was going out of town on business. Called my associates to handle business. An hour later, we were on a flight to Paris.

That night, we landed and took a taxi to the seventh arrondissement, the fancy district where the Eiffel Tower is located.

"One of my favorite restaurants," I told Billie, when we pulled up to a restaurant with a private elevator and a view of the entire city. "Worth traveling for."

I knew Billie ain't never had no one fly her out to Paris just for dinner. But she didn't let on. She was cool and reserved. It was as if she flew out of the country for dinner all the time.

"Thank you for dinner, Mr. Lucas," she said at the end of our meal. She held up her champagne flute for a toast.

"I figured you could take care of dessert," I said, clinking her glass.

"I doubt it," she said with a smile.

"Why the hell not?"

"Mr. Lucas, I'm a divorcee. Almost. Still working on the paperwork."

"What stupid fool let you go?"

Billie laughed out loud. "His name is Frankie. Works in radio."

Later on, I would find out that this was none other than Frankie Crocker, the legendary New York disk jockey from WBLS.

"And I saw you all hugged up with Walt . . ."

"He's a good friend."

"Well, now you don't have any friends. Except me. I'm the only friend you need."

"We'll see about that."

I hung out in Paris with Billie for a few days before we flew back home. I liked her. A lot. She was intelligent, refined, and sweet. And she seemed to understand that although I was a criminal, I still had a softer side. I didn't feel like she wanted anything from me except good conversation. We talked a lot, about her mother, Marguerite, who had adopted her before meeting Willie Mays, who also adopted her and gave her his last name. On the way back home, we made plans to go out to Vegas.

"I can't believe you've never been to Vegas!" I said, as we landed at JFK.

Billie shrugged. "What's so great about Vegas?"

"You'll see," I said. "You will see."

I picked up my car, dropped Billie off in Queens, and made my way back to Harlem. I checked in with my associates to make sure everything work-related was running smoothly. Then I headed to the River Bend Apartments. It was late. But Miriam was up, sitting on the couch, her eyes red. I knew I was wrong. I had called her when I got to the airport and told her I had to go out of town for work but I knew that she knew I was lying. I have to say, though, I really didn't care. Call me evil if you want to. But Miriam knew what she was getting from me. And she knew it before she married me and could have left at any time.

"Where've you been, Frank?" she asked, her voice shaking.

"I told you I had to go out of town," I said. "I ain't been gone but two days. Damn."

"Who were you with?"

"You must have me confused with some other nigga. I don't account for where I been to nobody."

"Fine."

Miriam got up and went into the bedroom and closed the door. I felt a little bad. Mostly because she was carrying my child. And I know women are sensitive when they're pregnant. I went into the bedroom where Miriam was on the bed, crying.

"You been back to the doctor?" I asked.

"You better believe I went to the doctor," she said.

There was something about the way she said it that threw me off.

"Is everything okay?" I asked.

Miriam sat up and wiped her eyes with her hands and gave a weak smile.

"Oh, everything's fine now. Just perfect."

Sarcasm was dripping off every word and I felt my stomach churning 'cause I didn't know what kind of point she was trying to make.

"What's going on?"

"What going on?" she said. "I ain't pregnant no more. That's what's going on."

"Shit," I said. "You had a miscarriage? Is that why you were so upset that I wasn't here?"

"No, Frank, I didn't have no miscarriage. I got rid of the baby. If you want to be out in the world doing whatever you want to do, I ain't having no baby by you."

I had to hold myself back from smacking the shit out of her. It was wrong. What she did was flat-out wrong. She aborted my child to punish me? I thought that was sick and disgusting and I could barely look at her. I knew I wasn't a good husband. But why beg me to marry you, have unprotected sex with me when you know you can get pregnant, and then get an abortion when I won't do what you want me to do? I was disgusted with Miriam and cursed her out for the rest of the night.

I left and ended up getting a room at The Plaza for a few days. Met a white girl with red hair and blue eyes. Her name was Anne. We spent damn near a week in bed at The Plaza. This woman did some crazy things to me, reminded me of Lucy Kennedy, the white girl from down South all those years ago.

I laid up with Anne for a good long time. And just when I thought we were all done and I'd get up to leave, she'd pull me right back down for another round.

Finally, she told me she had to get home for some reason or another. I swear to you, I think I'd still be there right now if she hadn't had to leave. She was one of those "I ain't never been with a black man" girls from Park Avenue who gets turned out pretty quickly.

After I checked out of The Plaza, I went to another apartment I had out in Queens. I took a shower, changed clothes, and slept. Had to pick up a package in midtown and then went on home. I knew I was going to have to hear Miriam's mouth. I just knew it. She was going to bitch and moan about me leaving for a whole week. But I was still hot with her for aborting our child, so I didn't really care what she had to say.

Soon as I got to the lobby of my building, the handyman, an elderly black man, stopped me before I could get on the elevator.

"You going upstairs now, Mr. Lucas?" he said.

"Yeah. Why?"

"Not sure if you should go upstairs right now," he said. He wiped his brow and looked nervously around the lobby.

"Why not?"

"I saw four detectives go up there just a few minutes ago."

"What did she do?" I asked.

"Not her. You. Mrs. Lucas came down here to the lobby and took them upstairs."

"Get the fuck out of here," I said.

"It's true."

I had two .44s on me. And a kilo of cocaine. I gave everything to the handyman, who went inside his little utility room.

"Hold on to this stuff," I said, slipping him a hundred-dollar bill. "I'll call you later to tell you where to bring it."

"Yes, sir."

I left the River Bend Apartments and never looked back. Never went back to that building again. And didn't see Miriam for twenty years after that. I heard from someone that she ran down to Mexico and divorced me. I could not have cared any less. I ran into her many years later and she came up to me all laughing and smiling, talking about, "I'm still Mrs. Lucas. I never changed my name!" I said, "Well, you should have," and kept on walking.

She really tried to set me up. And just because she couldn't have me on her terms, she was ready to get my ass locked up indefinitely. And if that handyman hadn't looked out for me, I might still be in prison right now behind that shit.

I checked right back into The Plaza and stayed there and out in Queens and wherever else I felt like laying my hat. I continued dating Billie, who was just as sweet as she wanted to be. And I continued working for Bumpy, though I was bored to tears. I ran my numbers spot, I sold drugs on the side, and I did whatever else Bumpy wanted me to do. I had all the money I could spend and all of life's luxuries. And it wasn't enough. It never would be.

10

A usual night at Wells' Restaurant in Harlem. Probably around six or seven in the evening. Wells' was a spot we went to often back then. It was a little café, maybe it could fit a hundred people inside. Sometimes we'd be there twice a week, other times we'd be there twice a month. But whenever we sat down at one of the round tables, the waitress didn't waste time bringing Bumpy his meal.

"Fried chicken, one waffle. Wing and a leg," said the waitress at Wells' one night as she placed his plate in front of him.

Bumpy smiled. Then he shook out his cloth napkin and placed it in his lap.

"Perfect. Thank you," he said.

"What can I get you, Mr. Lucas?"

"What's the special?"

"Lamb stew."

I shook my head quickly. I didn't eat lamb. Down South,

white country boys would use lambs for girlfriends. Couldn't see myself eating one.

"Let me have the veal," I said. "Side of rice and snap beans."

As we waited for our order, I kept a close eye on not just my surroundings in the restaurant but on Bumpy as well. The past few days he hadn't been himself. A few mornings, when I picked him up, I'd ask him if he was okay and he'd just say he wasn't feeling well. He didn't talk much anyway, but the past three days, he'd been talking even less than usual.

"You okay, sir?" I asked.

Bumpy took a sip of ice water and nodded. "I'll be fine once I eat."

That morning had been typical. I picked him up at nine. Then we went down to Al Cabell's joint on 136th and Lenox. Bumpy played a few games of Skin and I stayed nearby, keeping an eye and ear out. Bumpy went to a meeting. I checked in on my numbers spot and made a few pickups for Bumpy and then I picked him up again for lunch.

I think Bumpy told me to tell a few folks to come by Wells' that night because I'm pretty sure JJ was there. And Chickenfoot and Cockeye were there, too. He must have had something to tell us that night. Because I would never bring those guys to the dinner table with Bumpy otherwise. I had to have a reason to bring them around. They were loud. They got high and they talked too loud. Bumpy didn't have any of that nearby. But I do remember them being there that evening, so he must have requested their presence.

The waitress brought our food and set the plates at the table. Bumpy sat up closer to the table and reached over for a fork. Just then, his entire body started shaking violently. I jumped up and grabbed him to keep him from falling over.

"What's the matter, boss? *Boss?* You okay?" I screamed.

Everyone in the restaurant rushed over to our table, where I held Bumpy while his body continued to shake.

"Back up!" I said to the crowd. "And somebody call for some help!"

Bumpy went limp in my arms and I moved him to the floor to see what I could do.

"Mr. Lucas, I'm a nurse," said a black woman still in her starched white uniform and nurse's cap. "Let me see if I can help Mr. Johnson."

I moved to the side, next to JJ and Cockeye. I had my hand over my mouth as I looked at Bumpy on the floor. The nurse picked up Bumpy's wrist, held it for a few seconds, and then placed his hand back on the floor.

"Mr. Lucas," she said. "I'm sorry. But Mr. Johnson is dead."

Before I could even process the information, I heard the roar of ambulances coming up Seventh Avenue. Three of the ambulances stopped right in front of the restaurant and the emergency workers rushed inside and hovered over Bumpy. I stood there in silence, stunned. As they placed Bumpy on a stretcher and moved him to the back of the ambulance, I still didn't move. I couldn't move. I was rooted to the spot.

"You aiight, Frank?" JJ asked me.

"Hell no I ain't," I said.

The ambulance prepared to go up to Harlem Hospital. I followed in my car. I pulled up right behind the ambulance when they got to the emergency room. And I watched them take the stretcher out as I walked up. Before they took him inside, they took a blanket and pulled it up over his entire body, including his face. That's when it really hit me. There was no point in going inside that hospital. They weren't putting Bumpy in a room. They were taking him to the morgue. The man who had guided my life, saved my life, and taught me more than any teacher I'd ever had was now dead.

I left the hospital and went right up to Small's.

"I heard about Bumpy," said the bartender.

"Dewar's," I said.

The bartender brought the whole bottle and gave me a glass of ice. I didn't even touch the glass. I just turned the bottle up and took a hard swallow. The alcohol burned my throat going down, which is exactly what I needed. I was in pain, and I needed to numb it. Quickly. I threw the bottle back and took another swallow.

"Frank, slow down," the bartender said.

"Don't tell me what the fuck to do," I snapped.

He backed off and went to the other side of the bar and I went back to my bottle. I drained that whole fifth of liquor in no time at all. I barely remember the rest of the night 'cause I was so drunk. I vaguely remember trying to get to the front door to go to my car and then Pete MacDougal coming over and making me sit down.

"I got someone on the way to pick you up, Frank," he said. "Just chill out right here."

The next three or four days went by in a blur. Even the day of Bumpy's funeral seems foggy, like it was a dream. I do remember that Billy Daniels was there. He sang one of his hit songs. I'm thinking it was "My Buddy." You couldn't even get close to the church that day. Everyone who was somebody was there. From the common man to the criminals. All the mobsters were there, too. Some still alive today that may not want me to mention their names, so I won't. But everyone who was anyone in the streets was there to pay tribute to the great Bumpy Johnson.

"Lucas, need to speak with you."

At the funeral home, I looked up and saw Zack Robinson beckoning me to a small office inside the funeral parlor. As I followed him, I could see a few people darting their eyes over to see what was going on. He sat down on a chair near a desk and motioned for me to sit down as well.

"Bumpy told me to make sure you were taken care of . . ."

I just nodded my head.

"Bumpy's enterprises are yours. You know that."

I nodded again.

"If you have any trouble out of anyone, you let me know."

"Will do."

I turned to walk out of the office.

"Lucas."

I looked back at Zack Robinson.

"Yes, sir?"

"Do you need anything?" he asked. I knew he meant money.

"No. I'm fine."

"Just let me know."

It took me a week or so to get over the initial shock of Bumpy's death. I wasn't prepared for it at all and it just threw me all off balance. But I knew I had to figure out what my next move was going to be. Bumpy had over three million dollars owed to him in the streets at the time he died. And I knew it now belonged to me and I planned to collect every cent of it.

And then what?

All the numbers-running spots he controlled were now mine. I could get a few more people in place to oversee them and keep running them. I thought about that for less than an hour and knew I wasn't doing that. It just didn't appeal to me. For the next week, I collected Bumpy's money from the various businesses and numbers spots and, sure enough, I had over three million dollars.

When I'd first started traveling internationally, I'd started using banks here and there to keep my money. I couldn't get on a plane with the kind of cash I needed to gamble with. So, I got connections to banks with employees who didn't ask questions about where your money came from.

Through one of those connections, I was able to wash the collected money clean and deposit it in several Chemical banks out in Queens and lower Manhattan.

That night, after I deposited all the money, I went back up to my apartment to think. Three million dollars. That was an awful lot of money in 1968. And it was all mine to use as I saw fit. I knew it was going to be seed money to get something else off the ground. But I wasn't sure what I was going to do.

As always, I tuned in to the evening news.

I'm Roger Grimsby. And I'm Bill Beutel. And here now the news . . .

It was another report on the strength and easy availability of heroin in Southeast Asia. *Cheaper and stronger. Cheaper and stronger*. Again, the words flooded my brain until I couldn't even focus on the news. I knew what I was going to do with that money. I was not going to just keep shaking down businesses and running numbers spots. I was going to Asia.

One night I was on Seventh Avenue and I saw Zack Robinson. Out of respect, I told Zack what I was planning to do.

"You alright? You need anything?" he asked.

"I'm fine. I got everything I need." I spent more time at home for the next few days, trying to think about how I was going to make everything come together. First, I had to figure out where exactly I would go. The Golden Triangle that they talked about on the news was made up of four different countries: Burma, Laos, Vietnam, and Thailand. I barely knew where those places were. I bought a wall map and spread it out in my apartment, looking at the different locations and thinking about each one. Obviously I wasn't going to Vietnam. The war had been under way there for nearly ten years, so that would have been impossible. I could probably have gotten over there, but there was no way I'd be able to get my plan in place in a war zone. I didn't know much about Burma and Laos, but I had heard about Thailand. All I knew was the capital city—Bangkok. I remembered hearing that U.S. servicemen went to Bangkok from Vietnam while on leave to hang out, get women, and relax.

I took a pushpin and stuck it into the part of the map where Thailand was located. I decided that my journey would begin there. I planned to find a hotel once I got to Bangkok and then ask around until I found a spot where I could find U.S. servicemen on leave. If the news reports I'd read and heard were accurate, I'd be sure to find some servicemen hooked on heroin who could tell me where I could get my hands on some product to ship back to the States.

The next thing I had to figure out was how I was going to get the heroin back to the States. I was looking for wholesale product—nothing that would be on my person or on a typical commercial flight that would go through all kinds of inspections. I knew I would have to grease someone's palms to get the product back. It came to me pretty quickly.

Since I was planning to get a U.S. serviceman to give me a lead on a connect in Southeast Asia, I figured it would probably be possible to get someone in the military to get my product on a military plane and get it to a base back home where I could arrange for someone to pick it up.

As my plan started to come together, bit by bit, I knew it was risky. But I also knew that I didn't want it to be any other way. The bigger the risk, the bigger the reward. I had no doubts whatsoever that I could get over there, get a connection, buy heroin at wholesale, and somehow get it back to the States and into the streets. My name was Frank Lucas. I could do anything.

A few days later, I made sure my passport was updated. And I worked on making sure that all the money I collected after Bumpy's death was deposited in the bank. I had several people deposit the money in different accounts at different branch locations. When all the money was in the bank, I booked myself a first-class, round-trip flight to Bangkok. I packed enough clothes for a month. I wasn't coming back until I had my plan off the ground. Period. End of discussion.

11

I stepped out of Don Muang International airport on a day that was hot, humid, and sticky. I shaded my eyes with my hands and stepped quickly from the terminal into the street, where my face was flooded with the bright sunshine. I looked for a taxi and was ushered into the backseat by an attendant.

"English?" I asked.

"A little," the driver said.

"Where's the closest hotel?" I asked. "A nice one."

"The Dusit Thani, sir."

"Wait right here," I said, getting out of the car.

I went back into the terminal to a counter with a pay phone and a telephone book. I looked up the Dusit Thani Hotel and dialed the number.

The receptionist answered and I couldn't understand a word she said.

"English?" I asked.

"Yes, sir," the woman said in flawless English. "Thank you for calling the Dusit Thani Hotel. How can I help you?"

"Just landed in Bangkok from the States. Here on business. Do you have anything available?"

"Yes, sir. I have a room with a king-size bed available. How long will you be staying with us?"

"A few weeks."

"Not a problem," she said. "Your name?"

"My name is Frank Lucas."

"When should we expect you, Mr. Lucas?"

"I'm on my way."

"Looking forward to having you at the Dusit Thani."

I went back to the taxi with my luggage, loaded up the trunk, and got back into the backseat.

"Dusit Thani?" the driver asked.

"Absolutely," I said, taking in the sights and sounds of Bangkok, Thailand.

Now, before my first trip to Thailand, I had traveled internationally before. I'd gone to London and Paris just to go and have a good time. And of course I'd traveled to Cuba with Bumpy years before. But this was different. This was a business trip. So, while I stared out the car window, looking at the thousands of bicycles clogging the streets, my mind was not on anything but how I was going to make my plan come together.

I checked in at my hotel, went up to my room, and lay down sideways across the king-size bed. I was dead-dog tired from the inside out. My flight was not direct from New York. That plane stopped in London, Frankfurt, and Istanbul (where we stayed for a full day because there was mechanical trouble on the plane). From there we went to Beirut, Tehran, New Delhi, and then finally Bangkok. In twenty-eight hours, I'd seen the sun come up six or seven times. I was so tired by the time I got to the Dusit Thani that I couldn't think straight.

Before I could even contemplate my next move, I was out cold.

I woke up later that evening and ordered a steak, a beer, and a crêpe suzette from room service. I wasn't ready to risk eating at the hotel restaurant or going out to eat. I knew that the CIA and other government agencies from the States could be at a place like the Dusit Thani. I didn't want to arouse any suspicion until I had to. Ate my food. Smoked a cigarette. Sat in that room. And just let my mind run. I got into a zone I often go into when it's time to get something done. I can clear my mind and think of nothing but what my next step should be. I sat there for the entire day, thinking. And then I went to bed.

The next morning, I finally went downstairs, ready for business. I went outside to get a taxi and asked the driver about where servicemen would go. He gave me the names of a few places.

"I'm talking about black people," I explained, gesturing to my skin. "People who look like me."

"Yes," the driver said. "I will take you to the right spot."

A few minutes later, I was walking into a bar I'll call Richie's in what looked like a downtown area of Bangkok. As soon as I walked into the bar, I knew I'd come to the right place. There were dozens of GIs in there, hats cocked to the side, laughing and talking. To my left, I could see a guy picking on a guitar and talking to a Thai woman. The place was spacious, big enough to hold a few hundred people, and it was full of lively excitement.

Now, at this point, I'd already been in the streets for years. I knew a junkie when I saw one. And there were plenty in that bar that night. I saw some soldiers in a corner of the bar nodding out; I also saw a few who were moving too fast, and I knew by their jittery actions that they were probably high on cocaine. I narrowed down the crowd to the people I thought could point me in the right direction.

But that night, I just observed. I had time. No need to rush anything. I ordered a few drinks. Made small talk with the bartenders and a few people hanging out. I wasn't interested in making a deal right away. I knew it would take a minute for me to get the kind of deal I was looking for. A few nights later, I was back at Richie's, talking to a serviceman I had seen nodding out on my first night.

"This shit is ultrapure," the serviceman told me. "Ain't had nothing like this back in New York."

"Is that right?"

"You better believe it."

"I'm interested in getting my hands on some," I said. I was careful not to seem too eager.

"How much you looking for? I got a connect," he said.

"The question is, how much can you get?"

The serviceman looked me up and down for a minute. I guess he was sizing me up to see if I could be trusted.

"At least ten keys," he said, shrugging his shoulders. "Maybe more."

I nodded my head and lit a cigarette.

"Good to know," I said.

"Let me know what you need," he said. "I'll make it happen."

I had a few conversations like this with different servicemen over the next few weeks. No one was giving me the answers I needed to hear. Ten keys? Twenty keys? Hell no. I wanted a direct connect. I didn't leave Harlem and travel nine thousand miles to get forty keys.

At one point, a guy told me he'd get together with a few people and see how many keys they could round up together. I told him thanks but no thanks. Wasn't interested in getting involved with too many people. The whole point was that I wanted an independent operation. I wasn't trying to get mixed up with a bunch of people in my business.

One evening, I was on my way out to the bar. I left the hotel and waited for the taxi that had been called for me. Instead, a white Rolls-Royce with red interior pulled up right in front of me.

"Are you Frank Lucas?"

"Yes, I am."

"Let's go for a ride, Mr. Lucas."

The man looked white, but he had the eyes of an Asian person. Even though he was sitting behind the wheel of his car, I could tell he was pretty tall—at least as tall as me. Reminded me of Sean Connery, who I had just seen in the new James Bond movie before I left home. He had the same salt-and-pepper hair and he was built solid like him.

I knew word had probably gotten around about me. I'd been asking a lot of questions about getting a connection. My gut told me that my patience was finally paying off. I got into the car with no hesitation.

The man pulled off, and before I could even take note of the direction he was driving, we were out of the city and driving up a series of narrow, winding hills. In about ten minutes, he pulled off the main road and parked the car on a dirt road overlooking a tranquil body of water. We were now high above the city—although I had no idea where exactly we were. Which I'm sure he did on purpose.

"What are you looking for, Mr. Lucas?" the man said.

"No less than a hundred and fifty keys," I said. "One hundred percent pure."

"I can get what you need, Mr. Lucas."

"That's good to hear. Now, who are you?"

At this point, the man I would nickname 007 turned to face me and gave me a brief spiel on who he was, where he worked, and how he could get me what I needed. I can't share that information here. But I can tell you this: when he was done talking, I knew my plan was definitely going to happen. And it was going to be smoother than I'd ever imagined. He had the right job (and I think you can figure it out) to make sure I could get what I needed and get it out of the country with minimal problems.

"How much?" I asked.

"Mr. Lucas, one thing at a time," he said, starting the car up and steering it back onto the road. He took me back to the hotel and we arranged to meet again in a day or two.

It was time to talk money and work out a deal that was fair. In New York at the time, you could get your hands on a key for anywhere between sixty and seventy thousand. I knew that I was going to be able to get a price much better than that in Bangkok. After meeting a few more times over the course of a week, 007 and I finally agreed on a price: forty-two hundred dollars per key.

At that price, even when I factored in the money I spent in getting the stuff out, I was still coming out far ahead of anyone in the States.

"Mr. Lucas, I'd like you to meet a few people," 007 said to me one afternoon when he picked me up. We drove to a U.S. military base and he introduced me to a man. I know his name but I'm not saying. I'll tell you we were on a military base and he had eagles on his shoulders. That's really all you need to know.

After 007 made some introductions, we all small-talked briefly, not mentioning anything about why I was there. When we left, 007 explained.

"One hundred and twenty-five thousand for him. And he will make sure your packages are sent out on military planes."

I nodded. My plan had always been to try to pay off someone in the military to get my stuff home. But I wasn't sure how I was going to get to someone high-ranking enough to make it happen. I hadn't even told 007 that was my plan. I knew that it was better to do more listening than talking and that's exactly what I'd done. I kept my mouth shut, let 007 do the talking, and he walked me right into the plan I had wanted all along.

By the time my plan was officially ready to go, I had been in Bangkok for about a month. I told 007 I wanted 225 keys. I really wanted more than that, but I didn't want to scare him off. The 225 keys were going to cost me $945,000. Nearly a million dollars. I had all the money that I'd collected from Bumpy's debtors, so I was ready. I went to the local Chemical branch in Bangkok and had a certified check made out for $500,000—my down payment. I also got out the $125,000 that I would need for the man with the eagles on the shoulders of his uniform.

I gave the money to 007 and then told him I was on my way home.

"Your shipment will be at the McGuire Air Force Base the day after you return," he said. "Go directly to gate twenty-seven."

"I'll be there."

"Will you be back in Bangkok soon, Mr. Lucas?"

"You'd better believe it."

When I got back to Harlem, I knew I had to round up a crew to go with me out to the McGuire Air Force Base and bring the shipment back to New York. I only had a few people I truly trusted. One of them was Doc Holliday, who'd worked for me under Bumpy Johnson. I trusted him and I knew he could help me keep things running smoothly. But I didn't need him to go with me to pick up the product.

The morning after I got back from Bangkok, I met up with four guys who worked for me in Harlem. I had two people drive my Cadillac, I sat in the back. Two others were driving the U-Haul. We went over the George Washington Bridge, got on the New Jersey Turnpike, and made our way down to Wrightstown, New Jersey.

When we got to the base, we didn't go near the security checkpoint at the entry to the base. I knew people who worked for the military, delivering things to different bases. And I knew that they often drove around directly to certain gates, instead of going through the security entrances. I noticed the same thing at the airport: cargo trucks often drove around the airport and delivered luggage and packages directly to the plane at the gate. We made a left before we approached the checkpoint and drove around the base, along the road with high fences looped across the top with barbed wire. The gravelly road that rounded the base had gates in the fence every half mile or so. Delivery trucks and other vehicles were parked outside each fenced area. Obviously, some deliveries were cleared to enter the base without going through security. These fenced areas were marked with numbers and we drove around, following each one.

"What number we looking for, boss?" my associate asked me.

"Just keep driving," I said, my eyes on the fences.

Finally, we came to a fenced-off area with the number 27 on a white sign hung on the fence.

"Stop here," I said.

My driver stopped and the U-Haul truck pulled up right next to us. We waited, briefly, and then saw two men come to the fence, unlock it, and come out to where we were. No one spoke to anyone. I couldn't even see the men's faces. They simply walked to the back of the truck, each of them with large duffel bags on each shoulder. They threw the bags into the back of the U-haul and then went back to their trucks. Again, they each came back out with two large duffel bags and threw them into our truck. One of my lieutenants got out and gave the man a thousand dollars in cash.

Within sixty seconds of pulling up to gate 27, we were pulling off that base and back on the road. The whole deal was done in less than a minute. We went back up to Harlem and I directed my men to a warehouse I'd rented.

"Alright, let's get this truck unloaded," I said, telling my men where to put the bags.

After the truck was unloaded and the product was covered up properly, I led everyone back out of the warehouse.

"We're good for now," I said. "Deal with the rest later."

We all walked out of the warehouse, and I locked it up behind me. I watched everyone get into their own cars and leave while I pretended to head over to my own car. But after they were all gone, I doubled back to the warehouse and let myself back in.

See, the men I'd used to go pick up the stuff were not the men I trusted to really be a part of my plan. I would never trust them not to come to the warehouse and try to rob me blind. Then I'd have to go kill somebody, and that would be all kind of unnecessary messiness. I'd already arranged earlier that day to have my trusted second-in-command, Doc Holliday, meet me at the warehouse with his crew. And sure enough, as soon as I went back to the warehouse, Doc and his boy Glynn and a few of their people were pulling up to the warehouse.

I led them inside and then locked the warehouse behind me. Doc let out a low whistle, with his eyes wide.

"You did it, boss," he said in a soft whisper.

"You better believe I fucking did it. What you think I was gon' do?"

"We got another place set up for this," Doc said. "Apartment across town."

"Get moving," I said.

Doc and his boys moved everything out. They would take it to the second location to prevent the first crew from knowing too much about the operation. I always wanted to have more than one layer to my business proceedings. And with a project like this, it was even more important.

My work was now done. Doc and Glynn would make sure the product was prepared for the streets and sold. I didn't touch any part of that process. I didn't have to. I was no longer a drug dealer. I didn't deal with any junkies. I didn't touch any drugs, and I was several layers removed from the streets. I was an entrepreneur; I simply dealt with supply and demand. Some folks imported tea from China, art from Paris, or fabric from Italy. I imported heroin.

For years, I would use this to keep my mind off the guilt of what the heroin was doing to people in my community. Joseph Seagram made sure the streets had beer, wine, and liquor. And I'm sure he didn't feel bad about the winos and alcoholics in the street. Down in North Carolina, where I was from, R. J. Reynolds had tobacco fields everywhere. Made sure the streets were flooded with cigarettes, chewing tobacco, and whatever else. I know R. J. Reynolds didn't feel bad about folks dying of lung cancer left and right.

I was Frank Lucas. I supplied the streets of Harlem with heroin. It was my profession. And, like war, it came with casualties.

12

"Always good to see you, Mr. Lucas," said 007.

"Likewise," I said, climbing into his car.

I was back in Bangkok, just three weeks after my first trip. And almost all of my first shipment had already sold on the streets. I was back to pay 007 the remainder of what I owed him and re-up for the next shipment.

"Did everything work out for you, Mr. Lucas?"

"Perfectly," I said.

"And what can I do for you this time, Mr. Lucas?"

"Five hundred keys," I said.

"Not a problem."

This time, when I got back to the States, I had to go to the Fort Gordon Naval Base in Augusta, Georgia to pick up the product. I followed the same routine. Had a crew of people to pick up the product and another crew in Harlem to put it in storage and distribute it to the people who would prepare it for the streets.

Soon after my second shipment hit the streets, I heard from my lieutenants that different bosses from around the country wanted to buy direct from me. One of them, a black man I'll call Felix Jackson, flew out from Los Angeles to see me.

"Mr. Jackson is in town," said Doc. "Staying at The Plaza. You gonna meet with him?"

"Tell him to meet me at Small's tonight," I said.

I knew Felix through Bumpy Johnson. I don't know what business they had. But I remember meeting him and I remember sitting nearby at various clubs and diners as they talked business. And now, here I was at Small's, meeting with Felix directly while Doc Holliday sat nearby to watch my back.

"I hear you can offer a very good price, Frank," said Felix, while we listened to a jazz band.

"Better than anything else out there," I said.

"How much better?"

"Fifty thousand and two hundred dollars."

Felix smiled. "And two hundred dollars?"

"That's my price."

A key of heroin cost me four thousand and two hundred dollars. And I had to factor in my costs to transport it and still make a nice profit. I'd determined that I needed to make at least forty-six thousand dollars to make it worth my while. I wanted my full forty-six thousand, so I decided that my price per key would be exactly fifty thousand and two hundred dollars. I could have just made it an even fifty thousand dollars, but I wanted my exact profit—no less.

"Is it pure?" Felix asked.

I rolled my eyes. "Ninety-eight percent. Now how much you want?"

"Fifteen keys."

"That's seven hundred and fifty-three thousand. You'll hear from someone," I said. I drained my drink and stood up to go.

I knew Felix Jackson would have no problem paying my price. At that time, heroin was going for as much as eighty thousand dollars a key from people who needed to charge more because they had to pay more than I was paying. And you'd be lucky to get something that was 60 percent pure.

I became very popular. Very quickly.

By the time Felix got back to Los Angeles, I was hearing from my lieutenants that bosses from Milwaukee, Chicago, and Denver were inquiring about buying wholesale from me.

"Thirty sell in Chicago," Doc would say to me on some mornings. That meant we had an offer for thirty keys. I'd let him know if we could do it or not, based on how my supply was at the time. I didn't mind selling wholesale. But my bread and butter was selling in the streets, where the profit margins were higher. I had to keep my own operations running smoothly, first and foremost. I did not want to take a chance on selling so much wholesale that I wasn't able to keep the streets supplied properly.

Before long, it was time to make another trip back to Bangkok. I booked yet another round-trip ticket, updated my visa, and got in touch with 007 to let him know I was on my way.

The next time I saw 007, I told him I wanted fifteen hundred keys. He just looked at me and smiled.

"Not a problem, Mr. Lucas."

After my third trip to Bangkok, I asked 007 if I could see where my product was coming from. I wasn't sure if he would go for it.

"It is a very dangerous journey, Mr. Lucas. Not a vacation."

"I understand that. Still interested in seeing how it works."

He laughed. "Can't be satisfied with a good price and a pure product?"

"I wouldn't have gotten this far if I'd been easily satisfied."

"True indeed, Mr. Lucas," 007 said. "I'll see what I can do."

A few weeks later, I was trekking through the jungle in the dense area of Thailand that borders Burma and Laos. I had been warned by 007 that the trip out to the poppy fields would take several days each way. And that there was always the chance of things going horribly wrong. Needless to say, 007 didn't join me on the trip. He introduced me to the other men on their way and left me on my own.

As we walked, I felt more alive than I ever had. I had done exactly what I'd set out to do. I thought about those days I daydreamed about what I wanted out of life while I was working in Bumpy's numbers spot. I wanted to feel alive. I wanted to feel like I was in control of my own destiny. I was looking up, not forward or backward. And I had cut out all the middlemen. I was at the top of the chain of command, far above where I'd started out, buying heroin in a bar from Old Man Pop.

I'm telling you, I felt like we crossed every river in Asia on our way. From the Ruak River to the Mekong River, we trekked out on foot for miles and miles.

Finally, we got to a rock-covered mountain pass big enough to drive a car through. I went through and then looked out and saw flat land for as far as the eye could see. And across the land, there was nothing but poppies—everywhere. I was in complete shock.

Now, when I say there was nothing before me but poppy fields, you really have to understand what I'm trying to tell you. I'm talking about land the size of all five boroughs in New York City combined. And there was nothing but the poppy-seed plants—the plant that heroin is made from—stretching from one end to the other. I looked up and noticed that the entire field was covered with dark netting. The netting made it impossible to see the fields from the sky so that traveling military planes wouldn't know what was going on there. But the sun could still shine through and allow the plants to grow.

I asked my guides how the area had become the headquarters for heroin. In halting English, it was explained to me: in the 1960s, there was an anticommunist group of Chinese people who had settled near the border of China and Burma. They ended up getting support from the American CIA, which of course had their own reasons for trying to defeat communist China. The Hmong people traded in heroin, and with the CIA turning a blind eye to their illegal activities, the region exploded. They would use donkeys and mules to transport the product down from the mountains into the cities, where it would be converted to heroin and then sent throughout the world.

For my journey, I was tracing the steps of so many millions of people before me. Except that I was going to be following my package all the way to the corner of 125th Street and 8th Avenue, where junkies would trade their wrinkled dollars for a glassine envelope that would get them high faster than anything else on the streets.

I bought one hundred keys that day, directly from the elderly Asian man who had been instructed by 007 to take care of me. The workers there packed the product onto twenty-eight jackasses. And after a day of rest in their small village, we started our journey back down the mountains and to the city of Bangkok.

A few hours after we started down the mountain, I heard a rustling behind us. I stopped to listen. And the men I was traveling with also stopped, their hands at their sides, on their weapons.

I heard my travel companions speaking rapid-fire in their language. And then, through the trees, a group of masked men came blasting through, guns high in the air and screaming in high-pitched voices.

I pulled out my gun and started firing. I could barely make out who was who and I dove behind a bush to try to focus and make sure I only shot at the bandits that were trying to rob us.

I had my head down, one arm out, trying to return fire. There was yelling and screaming coming from all over and all I could think about was how far I had come and how it might all end right there in the mountains.

After a few minutes of exchanging gunfire, there was

nothing but eerie and intense silence. I mean, just like that, I heard nothing. Not even the sounds of people retreating. Just nothing. When everything cleared and we were sure we were safe, we began to inspect the damage. Quite a few of our men had been killed. The members of my team began to bury the dead. Even more of the bandits had been killed as well. They were simply moved out of the way and not given the honor of a burial.

We lost half the dope. And even worse, we lost almost all our food and supplies. But I was alive. And if I made it out alive, I knew I'd never need to see the inner workings of the poppy fields again. From then on out, I'd be happy to meet with 007 in nice, cool, air-conditioned hotel-lobby bars.

We had a long journey to make it out. And we had no food. By nightfall, the men brought back what looked like grub worms, huge and fat white wiggling worms that they ate raw. Just the thought of it made me feel sick to my stomach, even though they insisted that they were healthy and full of protein. Hunger eventually took over and I choked one down. Don't ask me what it tasted like 'cause I can't tell you. I just chomped it down enough to get it down my throat and swallowed it.

That night, I slept. And when I woke up, I was as sick as a dog. I had a high fever, a headache, and I felt like I had the flu. Looking back, I guess it could have been malaria. But at the time, all I knew was that I was deathly ill. And I was so hungry, I would have eaten a dozen of those grub worms if they had them.

While I tried to rest, the Thai men went out to the jungle for food. They returned with an animal strung up to a stick by its feet. I still don't know what exactly it was. But it looked like a dog or maybe a hyena. And it ain't look like no kind of meat I'd ever eaten. But I was so hungry. When they cooked up that animal, I ate it right down and was ready to suck the marrow out of the bones when I was done.

The Thai people put me on a handmade stretcher for a while, carrying me down the mountain until I was well enough to walk again.

And then we made our way out of the Golden Triangle and back into the city limits of Bangkok.

I could not believe I had made it out alive. I felt like getting the dope back to Harlem would be a piece of cake—now that I had my life.

Although the plan was to start getting the dope back to Harlem immediately—I couldn't do it right away. I had to take five days to rest in my room at the Dusit Thani Hotel in Bangkok before I could even think about the next step.

The whole time I rested, taking meals in my room, I thought about how close I'd come to losing my life. My whole life flashed before my eyes, the way they say it does when you have a near-death experience. As I recuperated and got my mind right, the trip started to feel like a movie, like something that happened in another lifetime even though it had just happened.

On the flight home, I was weak and still sick from the trip into the mountains. I must have lost twenty pounds. But I was still proud of myself. I'd started out paying other people for their dope. And now, finally, I was supplying them and making more of a profit than they'd ever gotten from me.

I'm sure I can be judged for choosing to sell heroin. But I was still proud of myself. Proud that I'd made it from La Grange, North Carolina to the city that never sleeps. And I'd done it on my own terms and was completely self-sufficient and self-reliant. That was always the name of the game for me. How can I be my own boss, make my own rules, and be the master of my own fate? Going to Asia had given me the power to do that. And though I had no further plans to actually go out to the jungle, I appreciated that I had been able to see exactly where my supply came from. It made the whole process even more real to me.

I returned to Harlem in one piece, tired and worn out. But richer than I'd ever been in my life. And on my way to becoming even wealthier. Not just rich. Wealthy. That was the goal.

13

"**M**r. Lucas, if there is anything else I can get for you, please let me know."

"My meals are already set up?"

"Yes, sir. I told them that they can leave each meal on the veranda and that you are not to be disturbed."

"Exactly. Thank you."

"If you do need anything. And I mean anything. Please do not hesitate to let me know."

I looked at the woman and watched her walk out of my cabana, switching her ass so she could make sure I knew what she was talking about.

I was in Puerto Rico for what I called a "backtracking mission," something I'd started doing when I began traveling overseas for my heroin connection.

A backtracking mission was when I took a break from everything and traveled somewhere—alone. I took all my meals in my room and made special arrangements with the hotel staff to not be disturbed. And then for days, weeks at a time, I would just think. I would go over every single detail about my life, everything that had happened to me from my cousin being killed to meeting Bumpy, to his death, to traveling overseas, to becoming a major heroin supplier.

Looking back now, I can see that what I did was to really go into a dreamlike trance. I watched my whole life like it was a movie, looking for any flaws in my character. Any mistakes I had made. Any smart moves I had made. And any hints as to what my next move would be. It would take me at least a week or so to just think about my life up until that point. The next week, I would plan. And whatever I decided to do, I made sure to set it up exactly how I'd envisioned it during my backtracking mission.

Puerto Rico was good for this. It was warm. It wasn't too far away from home, so I could get down there and back home quickly. And I didn't mind checking out the Puerto Rican women. Even though I was supposed to be focused on planning my next phase in life.

During that trip, one of the things I thought about a lot was my son and his mother, Jonita. My firstborn son had earned the nickname Yogi because he loved Yogi Bear so much that he would cry when it wasn't on television. Jonita would call me up and say, "Please come get your son, he's driving me crazy asking for some damn Yogi Bear all the damn time. I can't make Yogi Bear come on television and he doesn't believe me!"

This cracked me up. And before I went on my backtracking mission, I went over to Jonita's place to bring Yogi his very own television so he wouldn't have to share it with anyone else in the house. I couldn't make Yogi Bear come on television, either. But when it was on, he would have his own television to watch it.

When I pulled up to the building that day, I saw two boys standing near the lobby, nodding off. Junkies. I just shook my head and kept on walking. But for some reason, I looked back at the boys.

"Hey, Mr. Lucas," said one boy, who looked about fourteen. "You got a couple dollars on you?"

And then I recognized them. They were two neighborhood kids who hung out with Jonita's older sons, Yogi's older brothers. I had seen these boys in the neighborhood a lot and they were good kids. And now they were all a mess.

I had been in the dope game for years at that point. And I had never ever felt the least bit guilty. Why should I? I never told someone to shoot up. Never put it in anyone's hand. I just made it available. Everyone could make their own choices. I never touched that shit.

But I felt a twinge of something when I saw those boys all strung out like that. I know Jonita tried hard to be a good mother to her boys, but what about the neighborhood?

Heroin was everywhere. I left Jonita's apartment complex and passed at least a dozen junkies nodding off before I even got back to my car.

That day, I was driving an old beige Chevy Malibu that belonged to one of my nephews who had moved up north with one of my sisters. Sometimes, I took his Malibu out when I wanted to stay behind the scenes. I always kept at least four or five brand-new cars in various lots throughout Manhattan. But I loved sneaking around Harlem in that old Malibu. I named her Nellybelle.

When I drove Nellybelle around town, I could find out a lot more information. I was invisible in that car. No one recognized me. If they thought it was me, they changed their mind when they saw me get out of that piece-of-shit car. No one would expect Frank Lucas to be in a raggedy car.

Around four o'clock, I glided into a parking spot at the corner of 125th Street and 7th Avenue. I had instructed my lieutenants to make sure my product hit the streets at four P.M. each afternoon. I knew from my days dealing with Diggs and Pappo that the cops had a shift change at four. And the evening-shift cops always took their time coming uptown.

I watched several squad cars, marked and unmarked, heading down Seventh Avenue. At the exact same time, I saw the low-level dealers who pushed my heroin in the streets. They began coming out of abandoned brownstones and the lobbies of apartment buildings. They poured out of numbers-running spots, mingling in the throngs of people walking the narrow streets.

"I got that Blue Magic," a young man would say to no one in particular. Shortly, a few people would be standing nearby. He'd collect money, parcel out small glassine packages, and keep moving down the streets.

It's funny, I don't even know where the name Blue Magic came from. I might have made it up, but I don't know for sure. It was just one of those things that just popped up. And it worked. I never thought my product needed to be marketed. That's where the naming process came from—dealers trying to cover up for an inferior product by giving it a fancy name. I knew my product was damn near pure. No need for fancy names. But somehow, my product got the name Blue Magic and the name stuck.

I sat in Nellybelle, that dirty piece-of-shit car, and watched. The dealers who weren't selling Blue Magic were practically begging junkies to buy their stuff. My guys were having no trouble at all, which was good to know. I kept my eyes on my watch. The hour between four and five was prime time. First thing most cops did when they came uptown was get something to eat. Most didn't start patrolling until five. If the dealers could get the bulk of their product sold in an hour, it was a good thing.

I watched.

Saw a young man, couldn't have been more than sixteen, sitting in the vestibule of an abandoned apartment building. He had his pants around his ankles, his head in his privates, pleasuring himself. I shook my head in disgust. That's what heroin could do to you. I didn't understand how people could use the stuff. But that wasn't my concern. I was an entrepreneur. Not a psychologist. Not a social worker.

I saw a woman holding two small children by the hand while waiting on line to get product from one of my dealers. Her eyes were vacant and her skin was ashen and dirty. She didn't have enough money and started begging the dealer to cut her a break. He refused and she walked away sobbing.

I saw more and more broken spirits and sad souls trudging to get the drugs that would make them feel better temporarily. But I also saw my money—cash was being stuffed inside the pockets of the dealers on that corner. I was on one corner of Harlem. And as I sat there, I saw thousands of dollars change hands. And I had dealers on every corner of Harlem and beyond.

My sellers would be sold out, sometimes in less than an

hour. My product was that pure. No one wanted it if it wasn't stamped BLUE MAGIC.

It was surreal. A month before, I'd been in Thailand, seeing the product grow under the netting, hiding from the military planes. And then, here I was, standing in Harlem USA, halfway around the world. And I could see *exactly* where my product ended up.

Imagine Milton Hershey going out to Indonesia to check on the cocoa-bean crops, and then a month later seeing someone buy a Hershey bar in a corner store in Pennsylvania.

While I was in Puerto Rico, I focused on that moment. Was I really going to continue in the drug game? Did I feel guilty about it? Would I get over it? The answer to all those questions was yes. With that settled, I moved on to thinking about my crew and who needed to be fired or reassigned to a different duty.

The main thing that popped into my head was that I needed to be willing to go hard. I needed to not play it safe. I'd gotten to this point by taking huge risks. Nothing ventured, nothing gained. Going out to Asia had been a huge undertaking, something people just didn't do. But I did it. And I'd had no fear whatsoever that I could make it happen. I needed to remember that the next time a possibility that seemed crazy presented itself to me.

The trip was successful. After a month, I was rested and ready to get back to work. I had a game plan for the next year, a few ideas I wanted to put in place.

I'm sitting in first class on the way back to New York. It was midday, only four or five people in first class with me. One of them was a woman who smiled at me as she made her way up the aisle and sat a few rows behind me on the other side of the aisle. Cute girl, too. And every time I turned around to check her out, she was smiling at me. I didn't need any more of a hint. I made my way back there as soon as the seat belt sign went off.

"Where are you on your way to?"

"Excuse me?" she said, in heavily accented English.

"I said where are you on your way to?"

She just smiled and shook her head.

"Do you speak English?" I asked.

"A little bit," she said.

I rolled my eyes. "So this is going to be work for me, huh?"

"Excuse me?"

I laughed and the young woman laughed, too. There we were, for the rest of the flight to New York, trying to communicate. It didn't go well. I did get her name. It was Julie Farrait. She was from Puerto Rico and coming out to the States to work. It took me thirty minutes to get her to understand that I wanted her to give me the address of where she was staying.

"Ohhhhh, where I stay in New York City?"

"Yes, Julie," I said. "Write down where you'll be staying."

We went in opposite directions and I held on to the paper, not sure if I would actually look her up or not. Months went by and I still hadn't looked her up. I hadn't even really thought about her, to be honest. I was seeing Billie Mays pretty heavy still. And of course an array of women here and there as well.

The last thing I was thinking about was adding another woman to my harem. I was trying to stay on top of my empire, which was getting more and more difficult. As soon as I returned from Puerto Rico, I had to get on a flight to Thailand.

My enterprises had been running like a well-oiled machine. Doc Holliday, my right-hand man, had a crew of lieutenants who reported to him, so I was able to stay several layers away from the streets. I trusted my people to know that my product and my business were protected. And while there were other drug dealers out there, people like Zack Robinson and Frank Matthews, I was much more than just a simple drug dealer.

I had a meeting with Doc Holliday, my consigliore, right before leaving for Bangkok. Out of curiosity, I asked him how many forces we had that would hit the streets if we had to protect our turf.

"Between five hundred and a thousand," he said, not missing a beat. "All armed. Ready to hit the mattresses in fifteen minutes."

I nodded. I didn't need to know any of the details. I was confident that Doc knew what he was talking about. All I had to do was take care of my end of the deal at the very top of the chain. Everything else was completely under control. Doc had Glynn underneath him and Glynn had a crew underneath him. I knew it was all in place.

A few days later, I was back at the Dusit Thani Hotel once again, waiting for 007 to pick me up. He was late, which was very unusual for him. And he seemed to be slightly agitated.

"We have a problem with a delivery."

"What kind of problem?"

"Planes are getting harder to secure. Troops are pulling out of Vietnam. You need to think of something," 007 said.

"I will."

He steered the car and still turned his face around to

look at me. "You're purchasing five hundred keys on this trip."

"Yes, I already paid you."

"It's up to you to get it out of here."

One of the army generals we'd paid off a few times had left the service. A few others were just refusing our offers, for some reason. And then, just when I was struggling to find a plane to load my stuff, disaster struck.

A cyclone hit Bangladesh and over a half million people were killed instantly and more were missing. It was huge nationwide news and suddenly there was way too much attention on Southeast Asia, which was bad for my business. The military began sending relief on their aircraft, leaving me with even fewer options for transportation. I had a meeting with a man I'll call Lee, one of the few people I trusted on the Asian side.

"There's nothing, Mr. Lucas," he said. "Absolutely no way we're gonna get this stuff out of here."

"There's always a way," I said.

"This whole country is swarming with government officials. I even heard a lot of the big dogs from Washington, D.C. are here, too."

"No shit? Like who?"

Lee told me that one of the top-ranked politicians was there to show support. I'll call this influential government official Harry Harrison.

"Harrison's here, huh?" I asked Lee.

"Yeah, they're keeping his plane at one of the Royal Thai air bases until he leaves for the States tomorrow."

I smiled, a big wide smile.

"When you smile like that, Mr. Lucas, it scares me."

"You know, every so often, I go off on a backtracking mission to think. I backtrack throughout my life so far to figure out my future."

"Yes . . ."

"I was in Puerto Rico not too long ago. Told myself that when the next big opportunity presented itself, I'd have to jump on it with no fear."

"Mr. Lucas, I don't know if I would say that this is an opportunity—"

"Find someone on Harrison's plane."

"What?!"

"Do it. Find someone. And then get him to name his price."

"What if he doesn't have a price?"

I laughed out loud and then lit a cigarette.

"Everyone has a price."

The next day I got a call from my lieutenant. Someone who had access to Harrison's plane was willing to load the stuff on there and get it to the D.C. area for one hundred thousand dollars.

"Frank, I think this is fucking crazy," said Lee. "Are you gonna sit up here and tell me you're gonna load fucking heroin onto the plane of a government official?"

"Yeah, that's the plan."

"And then on the other side, we just waltz onto the base and grab our bags and get it up to Harlem."

"Yup."

"You're fucking crazy."

I *was* crazy. I knew that. But that's how I'd achieved everything up to that point. By being crazy. And not fearing anything. I was in so deep. Transporting heroin was a large enough crime. Why not raise the stakes? If I went down, I was going to make it worth it.

Harrison's plane took off on a warm, sunny afternoon as I watched outside the fence of the Royal Thai air base. As soon as the plane was out of sight, I went back to my hotel, packed my bags, and set out for my flight to New York. The person we paid off told us exactly which gate to go to at the fort and what time. They would make sure that Harrison and his staff were deplaned and that the plane was being cleaned and serviced before my men went in to pick up their goods.

I didn't go to D.C. Didn't need to. I went straight back to Harlem. And waited for word on how things went. Two days after I returned, I got a call.

"Done," said my lieutenant.

"Any problems?"

"None whatsoever."

"And you were worried . . ."

"I'm still worried. That shit was crazy."

"Hopefully we won't have to do anything that drastic again. It was a onetime thing. We'll keep it real simple from here on out."

"How come I don't believe you?"

All I could do was laugh. It was true. He was right not to believe me. I was drunk off power, and after bringing my shit over on Harrison's plane, I really started to think I was invincible. Forget for a moment that what I was doing was a crime and that it can be argued that it was completely immoral. Please just consider that I was an uneducated black man from rural North Carolina who was now a running a multimillion-dollar business.

If I was the head of Kraft Foods or Pepsi-Cola, I'd have been celebrated for what I was able to accomplish. In the business world, I had followed all the tenets: the laws of supply and demand, the concept of microeconomics and demand shortfalls. If my time with Bumpy Johnson had given me a college degree in the criminal life, then my years in Asia gave me the equivalent of a Harvard MBA.

14

Much has been made about me using the coffins of U.S. servicemen to transport heroin from Thailand to New York. My whole operation was even nicknamed the Cadaver Connection in the press.

Let me make this clear right now. I never, ever had drugs stitched inside the bodies of servicemen. I don't disrespect the dead. That's just evil. That idea never even occurred to me, and I would have never done it if it did occur to me. And I would not have allowed anyone else to do it on my behalf. Over the years, that act has been associated with me and I don't like it. I'm no angel. But I do have my limits. And that would be one of them.

But I did use false-bottom coffins. Soon after the Harrison incident, one of my people told me we were having trouble once again transporting the drugs out of the country. The numbers of planes were shrinking and more and more generals were turning down our offers. They were too afraid of getting caught. And throwing boxes of the product on the planes, attempting to pass them off as supplies, was just too conspicuous. We needed to hide our product better.

I was in a bad way. I'd already paid 007 for my shipment. And once again, I had to get it on the streets of New York as soon as possible. I had my lieutenants on the U.S. side waiting to distribute to the foot soldiers. It was a delicate operation. One screwup in the process could throw everything off.

I flew in a carpenter I knew from the States and told him what I needed.

"Coffins," I told him, pointing to the wooden planks I had assembled at an airport hangar in Bangkok. "Need them to have space at the bottom."

"So a false bottom?" my carpenter friend said.

"You got it. Make it seamless. Shouldn't be able to feel or see nothing that lets you know you can open it up."

"I can do that."

"We need twenty-eight of 'em. And we need them fast."

The carpenter and his assistant got to work. He put those coffins together as fast as we could fill them. They were perfect. They didn't stand out at all. The coffins were loaded onto planes with deceased servicemen who were returning home for burial.

I need to make this clear: I did not want to do this. I didn't get any thrill out of it, the way I did with using Harrison's plane. I'll admit, using Harrison's plane had me chuckling to myself. A poor black man from North Carolina using a high-ranking politician's plane to transport drugs to Harlem. That was a good one. But using the false-bottom coffins was an act of desperation. I wasn't proud of it then, and I'm not proud of it now. I've joked about it in the past, made light of it. That's how I've dealt with a lot of the decisions I've made in my life.

But deep inside, I was always conflicted. And the more time I have to give these decisions some thought, the more I realize how wrong they were.

I did what I had to do to get my drugs out of the country. Period. But I have to clarify that it only happened once. And I never did anything as disgusting as use human bodies for transportation.

I stayed behind in Thailand for a few days to take care of business. In the hotel bar one night, I heard something on the radio about a U.S. plane being diverted to D.C. The plane with my false-bottom coffins was supposed to land at Fort Benning, in Georgia. I already had a crew of people there waiting for the plane to land. I wondered right away if it was my plane that was being diverted.

"Your plane is now in D.C.," said 007, when I called him from the hotel lobby.

"I heard. What happened?"

"I don't know. But I suggest you get someone there as soon as possible."

I called New York and relayed the news so that my team could get to D.C. right away. I waited up for hours to hear back from someone.

"Frank, someone is on to us," said Doc. "They had that plane stripped down to the fucking insulation. They were tearing it apart from the inside out, looking for something."

"But they didn't find it."

"No. But they could have. This was too fucking risky. Coffins? You've got a death wish."

"Calm down. It worked, didn't it?"

"This time it did. Don't know about next time."

I came back to New York and took a room at the Essex House. With that latest close call now all cleaned up, I had a moment to enjoy the spoils of my hard work.

But that moment was way too short. I got a visitor at the Essex House. One of my few confidants, a man I'll call Rocky since I'm pretty sure he wouldn't want me using his real name.

"Tango's talking shit again," said Rocky.

I rolled my eyes and sighed.

Tango was a problem. And he had been for a while. It reminded me of when I first came to New York and robbed those big-time dealers. No one stepped to me because they weren't sure just how crazy I was. And then I got protection from Bumpy and they all had to lay off. I was having the exact same issue with a crazy-ass dude named Tango. Six foot six, black as night, and plum crazy.

Tango claimed he wanted to start selling. He approached Rocky about it and Rocky came straight to me. We'd already heard stories about him robbing other dealers or not paying back the money after selling his product. Somehow, he'd punked a few dealers who had been letting him get away with all kinds of shit.

That wasn't going to work. There has to be order in the universe, even in the criminal underworld. A person like Tango can fuck up business for everyone. He does something stupid and then people are after him, moving recklessly. Next thing you know, the cops are riding everybody extra hard.

"What the fuck is going on with this fool now?" I asked Rocky.

"One of our people gave him a key to sell. It's gone, but he's not handing over the money."

"Rocky, I told everybody to stay away from that crazy fool. I don't need that type of shit right now. I really don't."

"He's daring someone to do something about it. In the streets talking all kinds of shit about how you won't do a thing about it."

I rubbed my head with my hands. Now I knew exactly what Cool Breeze and the rest of them guys must have been feeling when I came to Harlem. I could easily go out and shoot Tango in broad daylight and be done with it. No one would report me and that would be the end of that. But you can't operate like that all the time. When you have a problem like Tango, you have to do something about it without the whole world knowing.

I ain't getting into details on how we handled Tango. No need for that. But I will say that Tango was only a temporary problem. Soon, I was back to relaxing at the Essex House.

I checked in and out of the Essex House as much as I wanted to, just to have another place to rest my head. I felt like I was always one step ahead of Johnny Law, so I rarely slept in the same place twice. I had a place out in Yonkers, I still had a place in Queens, and I stayed at the Regency pretty often, too. I had cars parked in garages at each home, at least a dozen overall, from a Rolls-Royce to several Cadillacs. I traveled wherever I wanted, whenever I wanted. I dated the most beautiful women, ate the best food, and completely lived a luxury-filled life.

But of course, at the same time that I'm running a huge heroin operation in Harlem, I had so much money that I had to have legitimate businesses to act as a cover. There was no way I could clear the money I was making and not have any real businesses to show for it. Just like Bumpy owned his extermination company, I began to look for a business to bring in a small profit and serve to wash some of the money I made in my criminal enterprises.

One of my first businesses was a gas station on 151st and St. Nicholas. Someone owed me some money, and they didn't have it. Whoever it was owned a gas station. I took that as payment and hired a few people to run it. It worked out well for a while—everybody needs gas. But when the oil crisis of 1973 took place, I had lines down the street for gas. The guy I had running it couldn't get his hands on enough gas to keep up with demand. We were selling each drop. But with all the rationing going on, it just wasn't enough. After about a year or so, I was out of the gasoline business.

My next venture was a small supermarket I opened on 114th Street and 8th Avenue. That one I built up myself. The building was there but I had it built out. Used all cash every step of the way. That was the way I paid for everything back then. Cash. Bought a Rolls-Royce. Paid in full. With cash. Bought a Cadillac. Paid cash.

Back then, a man named Big Jim was my right-hand man for all my legal businesses. He'd help me hire folks and keep everything running smoothly. We had a grand opening at the supermarket on the day we officially opened the store. We had the flags hanging in the street and all that. It was smack-dab in the ghetto. And I knew that just like a junkie would always need his fix, folks in the ghetto were always going to make sure they had some kind of food on the table. Opening a grocery store was a no-brainer. First year we were in business, I think I cleared about two hundred thousand dollars after everything was paid. Not bad at all.

Around this time, just about all my siblings had already come up and were spread around New York and New Jersey. I was happy to have my parents nearby and I was glad that I had a few legitimate businesses to explain my lavish lifestyle.

But there were some things I had to deal with. Running a grocery store wasn't my only gig. I was running a multimillion-dollar heroin empire that was bringing in a million dollars a day. I was lucky if I could get to the store once or twice a week. I had a manager, a guy I'll call Big Billy. He was half black and half Italian. He was doing okay as manager. But of course, I still had to check up on him and make sure.

One afternoon, I sent in an independent auditor to check on the store. Turns out we were two thousand dollars short on cash. I guess they thought since I wasn't in there every day that I wouldn't notice. But I'm Frank Lucas. And if you mess with my money, I will definitely find out.

"Everybody to the front," I yelled out to the store at closing time. The staff gathered, including Big Billy, the manager.

"I sent in an auditor this afternoon to check the books. Came up two thousand dollars short," I said. I made sure to look every single person in the eye. Some people looked confused. And a few people, including Big Billy, looked guilty as sin.

"You're all fired. All of you."

I sent every last one of my employees home for good that night. The only people I kept were my butchers. I knew they were back there slaughtering meat all day long and had little to do with the rest of the people in the store. I got rid of everybody else and told Big Jim to start hiring all new people. I had no room for anyone who wasn't going to be trustworthy. In every facet of my life, from the drug game to running a grocery store, I expected honesty. Anything less was unacceptable.

I kept my staff low. And I was never afraid to get rid of them all and start over if I had to.

When it came to the dry cleaners I owned in midtown Manhattan—I had to end up firing myself.

There was a dry cleaner called Ned King's on Broadway, between Eighty-first and Eighty-second Streets. I'd heard through the grapevine that Ned wanted out of the business and was looking to sell. I bought it outright for a couple hundred thousand dollars. He already had two employees working the front and a few more doing the cleaning and pressing in the back.

I'd learned from the grocery-store experience that it was good to buy a business that was already fully functioning with a good staff and good clientele in place. I bought Ned King's and only needed to check in once a week or so. Everything was running smoothly over there. So I was able to turn most of my attention to my main business.

And then, after I'd had the business going for a few months, my two front-end workers got sick at the same time. People were trying to pick up and drop off their clothes and were getting frustrated. I came in to check on things and ended up behind the counter when some middle-aged white woman with an armful of men's dress shirts came into the shop looking pissed off.

"Excuse me, sir," she said.

"Can I help you?"

"These shirts! Look at this stain. I just picked these up and the stain is still there!"

I almost had to laugh. I was a feared and respected man

throughout the streets of Harlem and beyond. I was running an international drug-smuggling ring. And this woman was wagging a pointer finger in my face over a stained shirt.

"What do you want me to do about these shirts, miss?"

"What do I want you to do?" she said in a huff. "Why, I want you to clean them again!"

"Fine," I said. I took the shirts and threw them in the back. I was running late for a meeting about a shipment of heroin coming in and I didn't have any time to talk about no damn stained shirt.

"Also, I need to pick up a few things. Let me see if I can find my ticket."

I rolled my eyes toward the ceiling. I knew I had an up-scale clientele at Ned King's. It was part of the reason why I'd bought the store. One of my clients was Eli Wallach, an actor from *The Good, the Bad and the Ugly* and *How the West Was Won*. He came in occasionally and so did his wife. I had quite a few celebrity clients. And I'm sure that woman complaining about her husband's shirts was some wealthy housewife. But I still didn't have the patience for her. Especially not that morning.

"I can't get any clothes right now, miss," I said. I started to walk around the counter to leave the store.

"Oh yes you can," she said. "You stop right there. I need to get my husband's shirts right away, so you get right back there and start looking because I'm not leaving here without those shirts—"

Now, this woman was just a tiny thing. Looked like I could blow on her and she'd fall out. And she was standing there with a finger in my face and her other hand on her hip. Her driver had dropped her off and had opened the door for her before going back to the car to wait. She was that kind of woman, educated and refined. And still, I wasn't who she thought I was. I might have owned Ned King's, but I wasn't her servant.

"Oh hell no," I said.

The woman's eyes widened. I remember she was wearing a full-length mink coat and some fancy jewelry. "Well, I never!" she said.

"Fuck this. You go in there and find it yourself. I'm done."

I got my keys off the counter and walked right out of there. Got in my Rolls-Royce and went right on up to Harlem. I never went back to Ned King's again. Couldn't tell you what happened to it. Left all the money in the register, all the clothes lined up in the back. Just walked right away from the whole business. It sounds crazy now when I think back on it. But that business was just such a small part of what I was doing at the time. If it caused me the least amount of stress, it just wasn't worth it.

I wonder what happened to Ned King's. Maybe the employees came back to work and took over the business. I have no clue. I only know I never went back down there again.

My next straight business would have to be more in line with my lifestyle. I wanted to invest in a company that was in Harlem, something that was already established.

I was friendly with Lloyd Price, a singer who'd had a lot of success with songs like "Personality" and "Lawdy Miss Clawdy." When I felt like hanging out, which wasn't too often, I might run into Lloyd here and there. He was a nice guy, friendly and energetic.

Every so often, I'd end up at a club with Zack Robinson, who was also friendly with Lloyd. Now, Zack and I went way back. He was the one who checked in with me after Bumpy's funeral to see if I needed anything. And I'd checked in with him, out of respect, before I went out to Asia for the first time.

Zack and I had complete respect for each other. We didn't hang out too much socially but we'd occasionally end up at the same place. One of those nights, we got to talking about how we needed a night spot of our own to hang out in and to use as a legitimate business. Instead of drawing too much attention to ourselves by using our own names on the club, we decided to invest a couple hundred thousand dollars into a place Lloyd Price was trying to get off the ground.

Lloyd kept the money off the door when he had his shows and performances but it was my place. It served as the perfect cover for me. Going to work was as simple as sitting in the audience and greeting people like Berry Gordy, who would come in with his mistress, Diana Ross, from time to time.

The Turntable was a good spot, very popular. It was in midtown, right on Fifty-second Street and Broadway. Everyone who was anyone in the music world would come to either perform or watch a show. I'll never forget, one night, Diana Ross got on stage and started cutting up, doing the James Brown dance and acting a fool. She was usually supercomposed so it was nice to see her letting it all hang out every once in a while. The Turntable was that kind of place where celebrities felt comfortable being themselves. We had performances from Joe Williams, Little Charles, King Curtis, Lonnie Youngblood, the Temptations, and, of course, Lloyd would get up there, too, sometimes.

A few months after the false-bottom coffins had been safely removed from D.C., I went down to the Turntable to check in on operations there.

It was a good night, a good crowd. I scanned the main room quickly. There were several couples on the dance floor, dancing to a slow song.

"Frank Lucas, how've you been?"

It was Melvin Combs, one of the few people I considered a friend. Melvin had just started dabbling in the game. I'd sold him a few kilos here and there and we ended up becoming friendly.

"Pretty Boy Melvin," I said, reaching to shake his hand. "What you up to?"

Melvin looked around the club with one eyebrow raised. "You know me," he said with a smile. "I'm just looking for some fun." I laughed out loud. "Slow down, player," I said.

Melvin was the kind of guy you wanted in your club. The ladies loved him, so he attracted a good crowd. And he was smooth and calm. Didn't bring a lot of drama. I've always considered myself a good judge of character. And even though I didn't hang out with him a whole lot, I knew he was a good guy.

After I talked with Melvin for a few minutes, I moved on to say hello to other folks in the club. Then I noticed Wilt Chamberlain, who was playing for the Lakers. He was dancing with a woman who looked like she was two feet tall next to him.

"Everything's going smooth tonight, boss," said Pepe, one of my workers.

"Who is that woman Wilt's dancing with?" I asked.

"You know who that is," Pepe said with a smile.

"No, I don't. Should I?"

"She told me she met you on a plane when she came from Puerto Rico. Her name is Julie."

"Ah, yes," I said, taking a few steps to where she was standing with Wilt.

Wilt did a double take when he saw me approaching. "Back up, big dog," he said. "This belongs to me."

"You scared of a little competition?"

Wilt made a big show of bowing down to me.

"Lucas, you don't have a chance," Wilt said with a smile before kissing Julie on the hand and heading back to the bar.

"How've you been?" I asked Julie.

"Excuse me?"

"You mean to tell me you still ain't learn no goddamn English?"

"I do understand. I just don't understand you. You have thick accent."

"I have a thick accent? You up here talking like Ricky damn Ricardo and I have an accent?"

We talked for the rest of the night. I got her to let me take her back to my place. But she wouldn't let me touch her.

"I'm sorry, Mr. Lucas. I don't do that. I'm Catholic."

Julie was a lot different than any woman I'd ever met. There was something about her that made me laugh. She was so green and naïve and innocent. We started dating and she never asked me what I did for a living. I think she thought maybe my parents had money. I don't know if it really connected to her. She was just happy to be with me.

Within a year, I was saying "I do" to Julie, at a justice of the peace in San Juan, Puerto Rico surrounded by her family and friends.

Julie was all excited about finding a place for us to live together. We started out moving from hotel to hotel. But she finally told me she wanted to rent an apartment out on East

Seventy-ninth Street. It wasn't fancy at all. Real ordinary. I literally had enough money to buy the entire damn building. And she wanted to rent a little one-bedroom apartment in there and thought she'd died and gone to heaven. I just shook my head and moved on in.

I liked Julie, but she was a country girl. There was nothing fabulous about her. Her clothes were boring and basic and not good quality. I had to get her fixed up so she could look the part of Frank Lucas's wife.

"Take this money, go to Fifth Avenue, and buy yourself some new clothes," I told her one day after we returned from the wedding in Puerto Rico.

"Where on the Fifth Avenue?"

"Anywhere you see something you like. And make sure you get yourself a new coat."

"What is wrong with my coat, Frank?" she asked, looking down.

"I'm tired of looking at it. It's old and it's tattered. Go. Shop."

"But I like this coat . . ." Julie mumbled as she left the house.

I gave her two thousand dollars, which at that time would be more than enough to put her in a new outfit every day for a year. Julie returned in an hour with one small bag.

"Here is your change, Frank."

This woman gave me seventeen hundred dollars back.

"Julie Lucas," I said, shaking my head. "Why are you giving me this money back?"

"I did not need so much money, Frank. I have new coat. New shoes. New dress. Many new things. And money left over."

I knew right then that my wife was not going to be able to know anything about what I did for a living. She was way too green to understand.

Soon after we married, I went to check in on my son Yogi, and I saw even more local kids still hanging out in front of the building, nodding off and begging for money. They looked like zombies. And there were other zombies all around that neighborhood. I was disgusted with the scene. I went up to Jonita's apartment and told her I was taking Yogi with me permanently. I wanted him to have a relationship with his mother, of course. But not in that neighborhood. By this time, Yogi was nine years old. He was intelligent, a good, well-mannered boy who had excellent grades in school. Jonita had done a good job, but I couldn't take the chance of losing him the way so many other promising kids had become so lost. His mother wasn't happy about it. But she knew there was a good chance of losing Yogi. And she knew I wasn't going to let that happen.

I brought him home to the apartment I shared with Julie and introduced Yogi.

"He's going to be living with us," I said. "This is my son Yogi."

Julie hugged Yogi right away to put him at ease.

"Come inside, sweetheart," she said. "Let me help you put your things away."

We ended up going to Puerto Rico to visit Julie's family, and after a few weeks, he and Julie bonded tight like glue. She even had him speaking enough Spanish to communicate with her by the time we returned from the trip.

My home life was coming together pretty well. I liked having Julie around. She was a good stepmother to Yogi. And because I was all over the world with my business, that was very important to me.

Julie was my wife. She ran the home and made sure things were going smoothly on the home front. But at work, a woman named Red Top ran the show on the streets for me.

I met Red Top through her husband. He worked for me in the streets back in the early days. I would come by his house to meet with him and many times he wasn't home but his wife, Red Top, was. And we got to know each other really well. She was from North Carolina, just like me, so we had that in common. I know Red Top's real name, but I ain't printing it. I hear she's a registered nurse now, living a good life. But wherever she is now, if people knew the Red Top that I knew, they'd never believe it. She was a black girl, cute as a button with red hair and freckles sprinkled across her face. And there wasn't nothing she wouldn't do for me and my business.

When the product got to her, it was raw, direct from the poppy fields. It was her job to cut it down, mix it with the quinine, and package it for the streets. When I first started out, she'd do it all herself. But, over time, as my shipments got bigger and bigger, she put together her own team of people who worked for her.

I never had to check behind Red Top. I trusted her with no reservations. And my people knew that whatever she asked for, they were to give it to her with no questions asked. I didn't even pay Red Top a set salary the way I did with some of my team. She took what she wanted off the top and just let me know the amount. There wasn't any amount of money that would have been too much for her because she was just that valuable.

You have to trust your chief dope cutter and you have

to keep them happy. They could fuck up a batch, make it too strong and kill people. They could also screw up and make it too weak and lose customers. Red Top kept everything even and running smoothly. She moved her operations around often. There was no one building where she would cut up. She usually would pay off a cop, about ten to twenty thousand dollars, and use his own home to set up and cut up a shipment and prepare it for the streets. No better place to set up an illegal operation than in the basement of Johnny Law.

Julie knew that Red Top worked for me, even before she figured out what I did for a living. I don't know if she knew I had messed around with Red Top occasionally, though. We'd started out as just good friends, for years. I truly thought of her as a sister. But before I married Julie, we'd ended up messing around a few times. She was an animal in bed. Couldn't get enough. I'm getting short of breath right now just thinking about her.

One weekend, in the late 1960s, I took Julie out to Vegas for a short vacation.

"Meet me at the pool," I told her, as she unpacked.

"I'll be right there."

As soon as I got to the pool, I scoped out an area for us and sat back in a chair, ready to relax.

"Hey, Frank. Imagine seeing you here . . ."

I opened my eyes and sat up straight. There was Red Top, sitting on the side of the pool, kicking her legs in and out of the water. She was sitting next to her friend Mary, who winked at me.

"What are you two doing here?" I asked.

"Same thing you doing here," said Red Top. "Relaxing."

I opened my mouth to say something, but then I saw Julie coming out to the pool area. She stopped when she saw Red Top at the pool.

"Hello, Mrs. Lucas," said Red Top. "Good to see you again."

"Good to see you, too," Julie said, as she sat down next to me. She turned to me and whispered.

"I thought you said this was a vacation!" Julie said.

"It is a vacation."

"Then why are your workers here? You are going to have a meeting about business?"

I watched Red Top get out of the pool and take her time covering her body with a towel.

"Maybe just a very short meeting," I said.

"Well, make it very short, Frank. You can't just work work work. You must relax, too."

I had no idea that Red Top was heading to Vegas. And that she'd be staying at Caesar's Palace, where I always stayed. I knew it wouldn't be worth it to try to explain that it was just a coincidence. And I figured the less I said about Red Top, the better for all involved.

Red Top continued to be one of the most important puzzle pieces to my empire. She could have taken me down very easily if she'd wanted to. And although she was loyal and had no interest in bringing me down, there were plenty of other people out there who would have been more than happy to see me fail.

Soon after that trip to Vegas, I had a meeting set up with Doc to talk about some wholesale deals. He'd heard from some people out west who wanted product, and we needed to discuss it.

My driver took us to midtown. As soon as he parked the car, I got out and shots rang out.

"Oh shit!" Doc yelled out. "Down, Frank!"

Doc pulled out a gun and started squeezing out shots on the car driving by. The passenger in the car had a gun hanging out the window and they were still firing. I leaped into the air, pulling my gun out at the same time. I got a shot off once or twice, hit the ground, and then rolled over.

Doc fired on the car several more times and then ran around to check on me.

I had been shot, right on the left side of my abdomen. I held my hand to my side and pressed firmly. There was blood pouring through my fingers.

"Frank? You okay?" Doc asked.

"I'll be fine," I said. "Who the fuck was that?"

"I don't know," he said. "But I think I got 'em."

I peeled my hand back to take a look at my wound. The bullet had gone straight in.

"We gotta get you to a hospital," Doc said, lifting me up.

"Hell no," I said. "Call Dr. Jones. Tell him I'm on my way to his office."

I went to my physician's office in Harlem and sat there calmly while he pulled that bullet right out of my side.

"I'm supposed to report this," the doctor said. "If a patient comes in with a bullet wound . . ."

"Yeah, but you won't report anything, Doc."

"Mr. Lucas, I'm going to have to stitch this up. Do you want anesthesia?"

"No. I have a meeting to get to. Just stitch it up as quick as you can so I can go about my way."

"When I'm done, you might want to go home and relax for a day or two."

I rolled my eyes. "Stitch me up, Doc, please. I'll relax when I'm dead."

"If you keep this up, you'll be relaxing really soon."

When the doctor was done, I went right back down to the club to have my meeting with Doc. I would have never gone to an emergency room. That would have gotten back to whoever had tried to kill me. And I would never give them that satisfaction. I sucked it up and kept it moving, knowing that I had to keep a sharper eye out for enemies.

In addition to watching out for people who wanted to kill me, I had to stay focused on staying one step ahead of Johnny Law. And at one point, I thought going into the entertainment industry might be just the thing to do to keep them guessing about how I made my money.

"Annnnnd action!"

"Johnny Cool, you know I love you."

"Yeah, I know, baby. You better love me."

"Let me show you how much I love you. . . ."

When Lloyd Price came to me about financing a movie he wanted to make called *The Rip-Off*, I didn't think twice about it. The producers only wanted a couple hundred thousand dollars and that was nothing to me. But when I met with the team putting the money together, they ended up asking me if *I* would play the lead role, a character named Johnny Cool, who was supposed to be the boss of a Harlem crime family. Yeah, not much of a stretch there. I was always looking for something easy I could do that would give me some kind of straight career. I thought making a movie would make sense. Until I realized that I had to get up at four in the morning every day to be on the set by five. They were shooting all around Manhattan and had special permits but had to film in certain windows of time. That shit drove me crazy. The acting itself was simple, I was pretty much playing myself. But when they started a sex scene, I wasn't feeling that business at all. I'd read in the script that I was supposed to be in the bed with some girl for one scene. And when it came down to filming it, I didn't like it one bit.

"Annnnnd *cut*," I said, throwing my legs across the bed.

"No, Frank, we need this scene," said Bruno, the director.

Bruno was full of shit. He was a big white guy from Texas. I knew he was full of shit from the door. He came to the set every day with the cowboy boots, spurs, and the skinny tie and all that shit. He was probably really from New Jersey. He just struck me as sneaky and phony.

"I think once you see it, you'll understand why we have to show the other side of Johnny Cool."

"I'ma show you the other side of your ass in a minute. I said cut. And that's that. Now, if you want me to direct this motherfucker, I will."

And that was the end of that sex scene. I ain't never been the type to have a bunch of hoes hanging all over me in real life. Wasn't going to portray that on screen.

I can't remember much else about *The Rip-Off*. I know we finished shooting. But I don't think the movie ever came out. I never saw it, anyway. I remember vaguely that I had another confrontation with Bruno while we were editing the movie. He wasn't cutting the scenes I didn't like and I ended up pulling a knife on him.

It was just four months of my life, but it felt like forever. I was very happy when it was over. I knew that filmmaking was not for me. I had written down the occupation "actor" on my passport all those years ago, when I traveled to Cuba with Bumpy Johnson. But I didn't know then what was really involved. I just thought it sounded cool. Well, I learned while filming *The Rip-Off* that there was nothing cool about it. And I was happy to put my short-lived career as an actor behind me.

I'd rather stay in the drug game and take my chances on getting locked up than take orders from a fake Texan in cowboy boots.

15

As much as I loved Harlem and all my little spots here and there throughout New York, I needed someplace to have some quiet downtime. So, in the early 1970s, I bought a beautiful five-bedroom house on a quiet, leafy street in Teaneck, New Jersey. Soon after we settled in, Julie became pregnant and hired a live-in maid and nanny who came up from Puerto Rico and had their own quarters in the house.

I'll never forget the first time my mother came up from North Carolina and came to the house in Teaneck to visit. I had always avoided all her questions about what I did for a living and mumbled things about owning property and things like that. I think she knew something funny was going on, but she hadn't started asking too many questions yet.

My mother has never been an easy woman to please. Not much you can do or say that would get her too excited. But one spring day, I picked her up from Newark airport and drove her out to Teaneck.

"You don't have the apartment in Manhattan anymore?" my mother asked, as she watched the scenery go by.

"I do," I said. "But Julie and I just moved into a new house here in New Jersey. Needed some grass and trees."

"I see you got plenty of that," my mother said. My father, sitting in the front seat next to me, just grunted.

"Look like you got all of North Carolina out here," he said, nodding toward the leafy suburbs as I exited the highway and began making my way to our street.

"Frank Lucas, I know you don't live around *here*," my mother said, her eyes wide.

"Why don't I?" I asked, a bright smile on my face.

"I know there ain't no colored folks around here!" my mother said.

"There's a few."

I pulled up in front of our house, a large Colonial with a half acre of landscaping in front. Looked just like something out of one of those fancy home-and-gardening magazines.

My dad got out of the car and stood in front of the house, staring. He scratched his head and then just smiled. My mother's hands went to her mouth.

"Frank Lucas, is this your house?"

"No, Momma. This is *your* house. I just live here."

My mother slapped me on my arm and walked up the lawn, her hands still covering her mouth. She looked back at me. I was talking to my father and watching her expression. She looked at me with so much pride that it made me choke up a little bit. She didn't know what I did. And she didn't want to know. But she was proud of me. And that felt good.

Julie came outside to greet my parents and my mother pulled her in for a tight hug.

"I can't believe it!" my mother said. "This house is beautiful."

"Come in, Mrs. Lucas," Julie said. "Let me show you around."

Now that I had the house, I felt like I had a safe headquarters for home life. I had Julie set up there, along with Yogi, and it was working out well. I didn't have to worry about her safety. The cops in that neighborhood barely let you turn a corner unless they recognized your car. I lived near quite a few local celebrities and they were all looking for the same thing: peace and quiet and a place to park the wife and kids. Teaneck was my home base. But I still kept a room at the Essex House and at the Regency for those nights that I needed to stay in the city for whatever reason.

But just like Bumpy had told me many years ago, I tried as best as I could to leave the street life on the New York side of the GWB. When I walked through the door, I wanted to be a typical American husband and father. Not a heroin trafficker.

Which is why I was very disappointed when an unmarked police car pulled me over not far from my house that cool, early spring day.

I kept my hands firmly on the steering wheel of my Cadillac. I wasn't giving this cop any reason whatsoever to blow my head off. I had a weapon on me and a small amount of drugs. I thought I might be able to pay him off. But I was surprised to be getting pulled over in the first place. All the cops in my town knew exactly who I was and would never bother pulling me over.

"Good evening, Mr. Lucas," said the officer when he got to my window. He smiled brightly, showing off all his teeth. The man didn't look more than sixteen years old. Had a wide-eyed-innocent look to him. But I knew better.

"Can I help you, Officer?"

"I hope so," he said. His smile faded fast and he pulled out a business card.

I looked at the card. He was a cop. And in a special division called the Special Investigations Unit. I read his name. (Though I won't print it here.)

"NYPD?" I asked. "Aren't you on the wrong side of the bridge?"

"I don't give a fuck about bridges, Mr. Lucas."

"What do you want?"

"Ten thousand dollars a month. Let's start there."

"Are you fucking kidding me?"

"My job is to bust motherfuckers just like you. You want to stay on the streets, it's ten thousand a month. You don't want to pay, you get locked up."

He stood back and looked at my car. He took out his flashlight and waved it into the backseat.

"Something tells me I'd find lots of interesting things in this car." He looked down the street. "And in that house of yours, too. Sure is a beautiful home."

"Where you want this money?"

"Eh, just get it. Quickly. I'll find you."

He tipped an imaginary hat and whistled as he walked back to his car. I was fuming as I drove into my driveway and went inside.

I was no stranger to paying off cops. We had a whole system for dealing with the cops in Harlem who were on the take. It was the price of doing business. Either your people got arrested all the damn time or you found out who you needed to pay off to get them bailed out quickly or never arrested in the first place.

But I probably spent ten grand a month on all my bribes to crooked cops across the city. And now this motherfucker wanted that much just for himself?

"Frank, feel my belly. I think the baby moved," my wife, Julie, said, her face bright.

I just grunted and made my way up to the attic, closing the door behind me.

In my attic, I stored all the large amounts of money. But never for longer than twenty-four hours. Then I would have one of my associates physically transport it to a bank in the Cayman Islands. (Wire transfers this size would bring too much attention.) I really shouldn't have had the money there ever. But sometimes, it was the only viable option.

I opened up one valise and took out a stack of one hundred hundred-dollar bills. The money was pocket change to me. There had to be at least five million in that attic that day, organized neatly and waiting to be transferred.

It was really the principle of the thing that disturbed me. That cop was way worse than the typical crooked cop. And that meant he had no code of honor or ethics. Pulling me over out of his jurisdiction? While in uniform? He was just as much of a criminal as I was. It was worse, in my mind. He took an oath to be honest and to protect and to serve. I had done no such thing. I knew it couldn't end well.

I found out that the cop who pulled me over was nick-named Babyface. And he and his crew shook down all the people who were making real money in the city at the time.

Two weeks after he pulled me over the first time, I saw the whirring lights and sirens in midtown Manhattan as I was on my way to dinner.

"Good to see you, Mr. Lucas. How are you?"

"Couldn't be better."

"Can I see your license and registration?"

"Yeah. Whatever."

I opened up the glove compartment and took out the money and gave it to him in broad daylight.

"So good to see you, Mr. Lucas," he said, tipping that imaginary hat once again. "Enjoy the rest of your day."

A few days after that, I got pulled over by a different cop.

"I've heard a lot of good things about you, Mr. Lucas," he said. There was a smile on his face that I knew was trouble.

"Yeah. What the fuck do you want?"

"Well, I'm trying to get a promotion. My boss is looking for me to bust someone big. He's got a picture of you in the office. I'll bet he'd love for me to bring you in."

"Are you fucking serious? You better talk to Babyface and get some of what he's getting."

"That's the thing. He told me to come see you. Told me you'd take care of me."

"Ain't this a bitch."

Within months of meeting Babyface, he had my crew pay-ing out obscene amounts of protection money. We had no choice but to pay it. But we didn't have to be happy about it. I was making so much money at the time that it still didn't really dent my pockets. But every time I saw Babyface's car on my nice, peaceful street, I swear I wanted to kill him. My wife was pregnant and home quite a bit. My son, Yogi, lived there. This cop was just breaking all the codes.

"What are you going to do if I don't come home one of these days you looking for me," I said to Babyface one Friday night when I saw him on my street.

"I guess go up to the front door and introduce myself to your lovely wife. She'd probably help me find you."

"It ain't even been a month. So I don't know what you want from me anyway."

"No cash this month. I want a kilo."

"You want a what?"

"You heard me. I want a key. I hear you've got the best shit."

The next time I ran into Babyface, he plucked a bag with a key of heroin right off my front seat and threw it in the backseat of his police car. A few days later, I came out of my home in Teaneck and there he was, posted up on the side of my car.

"This shit is ridiculous," I said. "You are way out of line. I gave you a fucking key. What the fuck you want now?"

Babyface picked up the bag and gave it back to me.

"I don't have time to sell it. You sell it for me."

"I can just give you the damn money."

"Nope. I like the idea of you selling this for me. You've got drug dealers on the street selling for you. Now I've got a drug dealer on the streets selling for me. I'll pick up the money later on this week."

I just rolled my eyes and threw the bag into my trunk. Obviously, I wasn't going to actually sell that shit myself. I was just going to peel off whatever cash I owed him and give it to him. But this motherfucker wanted to feel like I was selling it for him. And that shit pissed me off.

I started changing up my movements a little more. Staying in the city at different hotels instead of going home to Teaneck. My wife was pregnant and I didn't like being away from her. But I had to shake Babyface. He was getting way too used to my routine. And he had to know that he couldn't get at me whenever he wanted to. I was used to being invisible. Very few people knew where I lived. There were people who sold my drugs who didn't know what I looked like. I kept Nellybelle in a garage in Harlem and would take her out occasionally and survey the streets. No one ever gave me a second glance. I'd stand right on the corner, as dealers shouted out *Blue Magic Blue Magic* to passersby on the street. I'd be right there. No one would know that I was the one who brought the Blue Magic over, direct from the poppy fields of Southeast Asia.

So I knew if I could hide from all of Harlem, I could hide from one crooked-ass cop. And for a while I did, checking in and out of The Plaza, the Regency, and other apartments I kept throughout the city. I snuck in to see my family in Teaneck, coming in and out at odd hours and using a different car each time.

Two months later, there was Babyface, hanging outside the Regency Hotel on a Saturday morning.

"Where you been, stranger?" he asked.

I popped the trunk, and he took out his money.

"You need to find another sucker," I said. " 'Cause I'm going away for a nice long while."

"Oh really? I'm so sorry to hear that. Where you off to?"

"Don't worry about that. Just know that you need to find someplace else to get your retirement money."

Babyface laughed. "Oh, Frank, that's a good one. But I know it's bullshit. Straight-up bullshit. See you soon."

16

I had to stay close to home, Babyface or no Babyface, because Julie was getting closer to giving birth. One night, she got tired of me following her around the house, checking on her every five seconds. She sent me out.

"Go, Frank, please. You're driving me crazy."

I went out to Queens to a party. Got out there around eleven and called Julie around eleven thirty.

"I am fine, Frank. You have fun. Stop calling me. Nothing happening here."

I called her back at midnight.

"Frank Lucas, you stop calling this house," she said. "I am fine."

I got caught up in a poker game and then a few games of pool. I called Julie again about two thirty in the morning and her mother answered.

"Is Julie sleeping?"

"No! We've been trying to find you! She went into labor and left for the hospital. I stayed behind to wait for you to call."

I must have done 110 miles an hour from Queens to the Englewood Hospital. Double-parked the car in the middle of the street and ran all the way up to the maternity ward.

"Julie Lucas," I said, completely out of breath.

They led me to her room and the nurse put a finger to her lips. "They're asleep," she said.

"They who?"

"Your wife," she said. "And your little girl."

Sure enough, there was my wife, knocked out. Then the nurse led me to the nursery and I saw my new baby. The nurse took her out, brought her to me, and put her in my arms.

"Well, look at this little girl," I said. "Gotta give her a name."

"She already has a name. The mother named her."

"Like hell she did," I said. "Nobody cleared a name with me."

"Her name is Francine. I'm assuming after you . . ."

"Oh. Well then, I guess I can't object to that, can I?"

"No, you can't," said the nurse.

Now, of course Francine wasn't my firstborn child, but it was a little different. It was the first time I'd had a child within the confines of a true household and family. I had the twins when I was just a kid. I was never married to Yogi's mother. Francine was going to have the very best I could give her. Nothing less.

Francine had me wrapped around her pinkie finger immediately. As soon as she could say "Daddy," it was over.

Whatever she wanted, she got. And whatever she didn't even know she wanted, she got that, too.

"Daddy, Mommy's trying to comb my hair," she would say, running through the house to escape the comb and brush. She would jump into my lap and cry on my shoulder.

"Why would she do that to you?"

"I don't know! But I don't want my hair combed."

Julie would look at me like she expected me to help her out by explaining to Francine that she had to listen to her mother.

"Well, if you don't want your hair done, then that's that. Julie, don't touch this baby's hair. And I mean it."

Julie would throw her hands up and storm out of the room, muttering in Spanish under her breath.

It's a damn shame what I did to Francine. Spoiled her so rotten I'm sure her insides were green. If she didn't get her way, she'd overturn everything in a room. Rip anything she could get her hands on to shreds. And she'd bite you, too. She managed to turn out okay. So maybe it was all for the best. But boy was she a terror. All 'cause Daddy always let her have her way. Always.

For some people, having a child makes you rethink your priorities. If you're a criminal, seeing your children grow up might make you rethink your lifestyle. What if you died? What if you went to prison for life? What would happen to your children if you weren't there for them?

I didn't have those thoughts. I was thinking about how much more money I could squirrel away in overseas accounts. The money was piling up nicely.

The street money would come in through my lieutenants. Piles and piles of tens and twenties, fifties and hundreds. It was actually a pain in the ass to deal with it. And a bigger pain in the ass to count it.

The large amounts of cash is what really let Julie know what I was up to after years of her being clueless.

"Why so much cash always in the house?" Julie asked me one day, as I sat in a guest bedroom, preparing to take the street money to the bank to have it converted into large bills for transport to the Cayman Islands bank.

"Julie, the less you know, the better."

"I think I know more than I want to."

"Don't ask any more questions."

"I don't like all this money in the house. It's dangerous."

"I'll be back," I said.

Julie just looked at me and walked out of the room.

Over a few months, maybe a year, Julie got adjusted to the large amounts of money. She didn't like it. And she made that clear. But she knew there was nothing she could do about it. I came home one day with bags and bags of cash and she saw me emptying it out onto the floor of a guest bedroom.

"There's nowhere else you can do that, Frank?"

"Please don't start with me, Julie."

"Just get it out of here."

"Gotta count it first," I said. "As a matter of fact, why don't you count it for me."

"No way José."

"Look, the faster we get this counted up, the sooner it will be out of the house."

"Fine, Frank. I will count it."

I came back that night and Julie told me exactly how much money was there, down to the dollar. I couldn't believe how much faster she was than me at counting the money. I brought home more money, left the house for a meeting, came back, and she was done counting once again. Finally, a few weeks after I'd hired her as my at-home money counter, I came into the house and saw why she was such a fast worker. She'd hired someone to come help her count the damn money!

"Who the hell is this?" I yelled out, when I saw some woman sitting on the floor making neat piles out of my drug money.

"Oh, this is my friend Rosario. She was looking for work. So I hired her to help me. See, we work fast together, Frank."

Julie smiled at me like I was going to clap her on the back and congratulate her on a smart move. I took two steps toward Rosario and she got up real quick.

"I'm giving you exactly three seconds to get the hell out of my house," I said to the woman. "And don't ever come here again." I slammed the door and turned to Julie.

"What, Frank? She was just helping me to count the money."

That was the end of my wife's very short-lived career helping me out with anything related to my business. I went back to counting the money myself. I bought a money counter to help the process.

Of course, I could not have managed my business without someone on the inside at the banks helping me to wash the money. I didn't put any of my large amounts of cash directly into an account. I just rolled up to a Chemical Bank in midtown and I would sit in the lobby, reading the newspaper, while the people I knew on the inside would take my money, count it up, and then give me clean, crisp one-hundred-dollar bills in their place.

I had to pay two points on the money for the service. So, for every $1,000 I brought in to get cleaned up, they would give me back $980.

One particular day, after I got my cash, I had to deliver large amounts to a few different places. I had to give a half million to my lieutenant for overhead. Red Top had to get her cut. I dropped off some with my lawyer for him to take to the overseas bank. And then, there was a present I wanted to buy for myself.

A few weeks before, I'd gone onto Frank Sinatra's yacht. It was docked out in Nyack and one of the security folks was a guy I knew from Harlem. He gave me a quick tour of the boat. That thing must have been 250 feet, with a whole mess of bedrooms and bathrooms. The whole thing looked like an airplane carrier to me. The moment I walked off Sinatra's boat, I knew I wanted one for myself.

The day I went to the bank, I'd heard that there was an eighty-five footer that an investment banker was trying to unload. He had one buyer who wanted to finance it through the bank. But when I told him I was bringing cold hard cash, it was a wrap. That very day, I bought my first yacht. I called it *Mr. New York*. It was furnished but I brought in a designer to gut it and do it up in my style.

I used it as a hotel, for the most part. Instead of hanging out in a bar or in a hotel room, we'd go out on *Mr. New York* and hang out.

Had some good times on that boat before I ever even took it out on the water. Now, I'm not big on being out in the middle of the ocean. I like the water. But I'm not keen on drowning. I did want to take the boat out, so I hired a captain to take me and a few friends down to Florida. It was right after the Jets won the Super Bowl, down in Miami. We didn't go down for the actual game. But after they won, I heard about how much after-partying was going on and I was ready to go.

"Now look here," I told the captain of my boat, as we prepared to start moving. "I want to see land the whole way."

"Not a problem, Mr. Lucas."

"I don't want to wake up feeling like I'm in the middle of the goddamn ocean. Can you hug the coast all the way to Florida?"

"Yes, sir, I can."

I woke up the next morning, threw open the curtains in my cabin, and I couldn't see nothing but blue water. I found that captain and grabbed him by the throat.

"The currents, sir," he managed to choke out. "I did the best that I could."

"Well, obviously that wasn't good enough! Don't let that shit happen again! Don't think I won't throw you off this boat."

Somehow, he managed to keep us within view of the shoreline for the rest of our trip and we had a great time.

But Julie wasn't crazy about the yacht. "Too much attention," she would say, shaking her head. "Asking for big trouble."

After she figured out what I did for a living, she lived in constant fear. Would the police come and arrest her? Would they take away Francine? How would they live with no money? She worried constantly and I tried to comfort her. But nothing I said really helped to ease her fear.

The only extravagance that Julie truly enjoyed was a

place I bought down in Oxford, North Carolina that I named Frank Lucas's Paradise Valley. I bought two places down South. One had about four thousand acres and the other was over six hundred acres.

I'm a country boy, through and through. And of all the places I owned, Paradise Valley was probably my favorite. It really was paradise. I had about two hundred acres of farm-land. Mainly tobacco and corn growing there. Had a man named Clyde Coburn running the whole place. For some reason, we called him Sam. Sam and his family lived on the property and he and his staff tended to everything.

I put a trailer for myself on the place with three bedrooms— a master bedroom and two smaller bedrooms. I could have built a big old house on the property but I didn't want to. When I was there, I wanted to be a little bit closer to the actual land. The double-wide trailer was perfect. Bought it from Goldsboro and had it delivered right onto the property.

Sometimes I would fly down alone, just for the night, to regroup and think. Many times, I brought Julie and Francine and Yogi down for a week or longer in the summer. I had four man-made ponds stocked with all kinds of fish. I'd take the kids fishing and we'd swim and eat meals made from food harvested from my farm.

I also had six hundred Black Angus cows. Beautiful, ma-jestic animals. Francine would start saying *mooooo* as soon as we got off the plane because she couldn't wait to see the cows. Had a few breeding bulls, too.

There was one incident that took place on my farm that doesn't sit right with me to this very day.

I had this cow I had raised from a calf. Jet-black thing I named Sambo. For some reason or another, he became more of a pet. Other cows his age were butchered and eaten. But I had Sambo drinking beer out of a can in my hand and I fed him all kinds of snacks. As soon as I came onto the property, he was right there, nosing into my hand like a dog instead of a cow. I neutered the cow, same as you would a dog or a cat that you want tame enough to be a house pet.

And then, for some reason, when it was butchering season, I put Sambo in the pen with the other animals to be killed. I'm not sure why. I mean, I had cows there to be used for meat and leather. But Sambo had become more of a pet. But in one instant, when I was on my way back to New York, I thought it made sense to tell Sam to kill Sambo and have him ready to eat when I came back down a week later with the family.

A week later, Julie, her parents, Francine, Yogi, my parents, and a few other family members were all sitting around the dining-room table in my trailer. The cook on the property started bringing out all the food, a huge simmering crock of beef stew with potatoes and carrots, some burgers and hot-dogs for the kids, and several huge steaks for the adults.

Something in the pit of my stomach turned when I looked at the meat.

What had I done? That meat in front of me was Sambo. A cow I'd neutered and coddled like a child! I'd fed him out of my hand and would scratch him behind his ears for twenty minutes at a time. I felt like I was about to throw up as I watched my family prepare to pierce their food with forks and knives and eat poor Sambo.

"Don't touch this food," I said.

My wife had a piece of meat two inches away from her mouth. "Is it spoiled, Frank?"

"Just don't touch it!" I said.

The cook came over to ask what was wrong.

"Get this meat out of here! Right now!"

While the cook cleared the table, my family looked around, confused. There was no way I was going to eat Sambo. Just no way.

I truly believe the devil got into me and told me to kill that cow. Ain't no other way I could ever understand what made me do it. It was wrong. And I couldn't even look at that meat.

My family must have thought I was crazy. We just had vegetables and other side dishes.

My conscience was starting to fuck with me. I'd killed Sambo. And it hurt me. I'd done some heartless things at that point in my life, all without thinking twice. But killing Sambo threw me off. And I felt the emotion so strong that I still feel it today. And from that point on, I started looking at things differently. In what other ways was I doing wrong? And at forty-something years old, was I really in a position to start over?

17

It was easy to forget about the devil and Sambo when I was back in New York, listening to The Temptations doing all their hits at the Cocacabana. I was there with a woman named Betty. Betty and I went way back. We'd messed around here and there but never got too serious. She did have a child by me, a son we'd named Frankie. And I was still cool with her. We didn't have a traditional relationship. But she understood what it was. When I could and when I felt like it, we'd hang out and see a show. And I saw my son Frankie as often as I could.

That night, we met up at Cocacabana. I remember Dennis Edwards was there that night. Dennis was a good friend of mine. At the time, he was a singer with an incredible voice, trying to make it in the music industry. He really wanted to become a member of The Temptations, the group performing that night, and he wouldn't stop talking about it all evening.

Eddie Kendricks, the lead singer of the group back then, came down to see me at my table after the show.

"Nice to see you, Mr. Lucas," he said, shaking my hand.

"Good show you put on tonight," I said.

I'd heard through the grapevine that he was mainly up in my face 'cause he wanted some coke and I guess he thought maybe I'd hook him up. I didn't touch the stuff. But I told whoever I was with that night to give him whatever he wanted. I was feeling charitable. 'Cause usually, I didn't let anyone use anything I had for free. I didn't care who they were.

Sammy Davis Jr. was the headliner that night. And no one puts on a show like Sammy. No one. I had a good time. I took Betty home, and instead of going straight home, I think I stayed at one of my places in the city. I had a meeting about a shipment coming into one of the bases and I needed to talk with Doc and Glynn about the logistics.

But that morning, Doc called me about something completely different.

"Your number came up, Frank."

I yawned and sat up in bed. "No shit."

"Yup. Four eight five. How much did you play?"

"Let me think. Oh shit."

I remembered right away that for some reason, I'd played a lot more than usual that night. I just had a feeling and wanted to go with it. I wanted to put a thousand dollars on 485. I always played the numbers. But every once in a while, I played a real large amount. Not too often, just once in a while, when I had the feeling. I couldn't find any runners who would let me play a thousand, though. No one wanted to take a bet that large. So I ended up playing $200 with one person, $300 with another, and then another $200 with a third bookie. I'd played $700 and the odds were six to one. Just like that, I'd won $420,000. Damn near a half million.

The crazy thing is, that still wasn't a lot of money for me. I remember going around to the bookies, who each gave me tightly packed brown bags with hundreds of thousands of dollars neatly contained inside. I put the money into the trunk of one of my cars.

And then, I swear to God, I forgot all about it. I literally forgot that I had a half-million dollars in my car. I drove around for months with that money in the car.

Finally, Julie drove my car one day to do some shopping and found the money. If it weren't for her bugging me about it, I don't know if I would have ever remembered to take that money out and add it to the piles of money headed to my overseas account.

That just shows how I was living at that time. Money was my motivation. But it was overflowing so much that it almost didn't feel real to me. There was nothing I couldn't have. I could buy pretty much anything I wanted. I had mansions, apartments. I'd even bought office buildings in Chicago, Detroit, and Los Angeles. Every time I visited my wife's family in Puerto Rico, I ended up buying some property. In addition to being a major supplier of heroin, I was also becoming a real estate mogul as well. I quietly invested in deals and fronted money for legitimate businesses whenever I could.

By 1974, I had easily made a half-billion dollars. Money was nothing to me. Nothing at all.

"I want a private plane," I told Julie one day over dinner.

"No, Frank. No," she said, shaking her head vigorously. "No!"

"I need to get to certain locations without dealing with customs and waiting on lines and all that shit."

"Too much attention, Frank. You don't think people will wonder how you own a plane?"

"I'm a businessman."

"Right, Frank. A businessman. No planes. Please."

I looked into it anyway. A private plane would cost me a half-million dollars. I asked around and looked at the numbers and realized that I could do it. And I could then put enough away to live well for many many years. I started thinking about getting a plane and then getting out of the game. Just get enough money to get the plane and stuff my accounts with cash. I could retire in style and live well for the rest of my life on the money I had.

In the meantime, I had to make sure my family was well taken care of as well. Several of my siblings had been migrating to New York from down South, like millions of other black folks. I would do all I could to help them get settled. I didn't want them going into my line of work. But if they needed help finding work or a job, I was right there for them.

One of my sisters had a son named Pop. I liked my nephew. He was smart and very athletic, just as I had been. And he could play third base like Brooks Robinson. Whenever the family hung out for gatherings in Paradise Valley, I noticed that he was beyond just good. He had something really special. It was really an amazing thing to see. I saw him play Little League and some high-school games and it was electrifying.

"You think I could play in the majors, Uncle Frank?" Pop said to me one afternoon, his bat on his shoulder as always.

"I don't think you could. I know you could. That's a fact."

"I'd rather work for you, Uncle Frank."

"Work for me doing what?"

"Uncle Frank, I'm not an idiot. I know who you are. I know what you do. Everybody in Harlem knows who you are. My last name is Lucas and I'm practically a celebrity just for being related to you."

"You ain't got no business in my line of work. I have different plans for you."

"But I want to—"

"I'm not talking about it anymore, Pop. Work on your hit. Work on your pitch. You got something special there. Try out for one of the majors. I'm not lying when I say I think you got what it takes."

"Yeah, I guess so."

Just a few weeks later, I was at a Yankees' game with my brother Larry. The Yankees were playing an exhibition game with the Giants. Larry and I ended up sitting next to Michael Burke, the president of the Yankees at the time, and Horace Stoneham, the owner of the Giants, whom we both knew pretty well.

"Mr. Lucas, you know any good ball players?" Michael Burke said to me.

"My nephew," I said. "He's just as good as anyone out on the field today."

"That's a bold statement," Michael Burke said.

"It's bold. And it's true. My nephew is phenomenal."

"Well then, maybe we should take a look at him," he said.

"Are they doing tryouts anytime soon?"

"Don't have to be. We can shut the stadium down and just let your nephew show his stuff."

"I'd appreciate that."

A few weeks later, we had a private audition set up. It would be just a few people from the front office watching Pop pitch and hit a few balls. I knew without a doubt that they would sign him up. The boy was fast. And he could hit that ball out of the park without even thinking about it. I told Pop about it and he seemed excited.

"No one else is going to be there, Uncle Frank?"

"They're shutting down the whole park just to watch you play. So don't come in there with no bullshit."

"I'll be there. But, Uncle Frank, I'm still trying to work with you . . . in your other business."

"No, you're not going that way. I'm doing it so you don't have to. Make something better out of yourself."

"Uncle Frank, seems like you're doing pretty good."

"Be at Yankee Stadium next Wednesday. Eleven o'clock."

"I'll be there."

That Wednesday, I sat in the stands, high above the pitcher's mound, with my brother Larry and Michael Burke. It was strange to be at the stadium while it was empty and so quiet. I made small talk with Michael while we waited for Pop.

"I've been hearing really good things about your nephew, Mr. Lucas."

"He's amazing. Good kid, too."

Michael quickly looked at his watch and then smiled at me.

"Can't wait to see him in action."

"Pretty sure he's on his way."

Twenty minutes passed. And Pop had still not arrived.

"He was really excited about this opportunity. I'm sure he's coming down here . . ." I said.

"I have a few more minutes," said Michael.

Larry and I exchanged nervous looks. I couldn't imagine what might have happened to Pop. But who blows off a private audition with the Yankees?

After another half hour, Michael said he had to go.

"I'm sorry this didn't work out, Mr. Lucas. Best of luck to your nephew."

He didn't say anything about rearranging the visit. I knew he was pissed off and wouldn't even consider it. I'd wasted his time. If I were him, I'd never want to give Pop a second chance, either. After Michael made his way down out of the stands and out of the stadium, I stayed a little longer with Larry.

"Pop's been telling me that he just wants to do what I do," I said.

"I think he's already started," my brother said.

"What?"

Larry nodded. "Yeah, Frank. He's out there hustling. If your last name's Lucas, it's really easy to get in the game in Harlem."

"I told that boy . . ."

"Frank. Could anyone have told you to do things differently when you came up here? People told you to get a job as a porter on a train or an elevator operator. You weren't going to do that shit. So why do you think you can tell Pop what to do?"

"Well, I know I didn't have an uncle who could get me a fucking private tryout with the goddamn Yankees."

Larry stood up and put on his jacket.

"Don't matter. A man's going to do what he feels like he needs to do."

"Well, what I need to do is kick that little boy's ass."

It turns out that Pop did blow off the audition because he was running deep in the streets. I don't know why he couldn't just try out and see what happened. Hell, if he didn't make it, he could have gone back to doing dirty; I wouldn't have been able to stop him. But why not try? Jesus. I could have killed that kid. I could have choked him.

But my brother was right. I couldn't force him to do anything. He was headstrong and stubborn, just as I had been at eighteen. Hell, by eighteen, I'd broken just about every law ever written and some that had to be written because of me. But I didn't want the Lucas legacy to be about heroin. What were future generations of Lucas boys going to do? Keep trying to sneak into the business I'd established? There was more to life than selling drugs. Even I knew that.

And then again, what kind of example was I setting? I was still knee-deep in the game. All I wanted was my private plane. Then I'd retire and show Pop and all my siblings and my nephews a completely different way of life.

Just wanted to get my hands on my plane. Then I'd be done with the game.

18

Frank Lucas, that is the sorriest punch I've ever seen in my life."

I continued throwing punches, lightning fast, while dancing around the ring on my toes.

"You keep talking about going back into the ring," I said. "But if you can't catch me, Joe, maybe you'd better stay retired."

"You talking a lot of shit, Frank Lucas. A whole lot of shit."

If Joe Louis was in town, he'd likely be at Stillman's Gym or another one over on 116th Street and 8th Avenue. I'd always take some time out of my day to go check him out. Ever since Bumpy introduced us years ago at that bar, I'd stayed in touch with him, and he was a good friend. He'd known me for so long that I could just relax and be myself around him. I'm sure Joe knew what I did for a living but we never discussed it. I didn't get him mixed up in that part of my life-style.

"I could have been a prizefighter, too," I said to Joe, as I ducked his fist.

"That's what they all say," he said, laughing.

I finally caught him, right on the chin.

"Oh shit, Joe. You okay?"

Joe rubbed his chin. "Good one, Frank. Real good one."

We took off the gloves and headed out to lunch.

"Got myself into a bit of trouble with the government, Frank," Joe said, his face long.

"What kind of trouble?"

"Damn taxes. Back taxes on money I don't even remember earning."

Joe Louis had donated entire purses to the American government to use in the war effort. And now they were threatening to lock him up—this American hero!—because of some damn back taxes. This was one of the reasons why I lived a criminal lifestyle. Seemed to me like being kind and generous only got you smacked in the face.

"How much do you need?"

"Fifty grand."

"Done," I said. "Don't think about it again."

"I can't thank you enough."

"No, it's this country that can't thank you enough. And next time don't wait so long to let me know you need help."

"When are you coming out to Vegas?" Joe asked.

"I'll be out there this weekend. Bringing the wife and her mother and the kids. Need a break. We're going to Hawaii. Making a stop for the weekend in Vegas. You gon' be at Caesar's Palace?"

"Absolutely," Joe said. "And I can't wait to see the family."

Joe worked as a greeter at Caesar's Palace. He had such a warm personality and was beloved by so many that people liked to see him right out in front. He would chat with celebrities, gamble with other people's money, and take pictures and sign autographs for fans. He was the reason why I stayed at Caesar's almost exclusively when I went to Vegas.

The whole family flew out to Vegas that weekend and we did it up. I must have had eight or ten suites on one half of an entire floor of the hotel, all for my family. Even Francine and Yogi had their very own suite.

"What are we going to do tonight?" Julie asked me on our first night in Vegas.

"I'm feeling lucky tonight. I'm going down to the black-jack table."

"I don't want to gamble. I'm staying in."

"Don't forget, we're having breakfast in the morning with Joe and his wife," I told Julie as I left the suite.

I went downstairs to get started on my night of gambling. As soon as I sat down at the blackjack table, they started turning up the chairs around me to signify that no one was to sit down at my table. I had the entire table to myself. I was just about to place my bet when I heard the familiar, throaty voice of a woman behind me.

"Hello there, Mr. Lucas."

I stopped, my hand in midair, and turned around. Ena Hartmann was standing there, looking like the Queen of Sheba. Ena was an actress I'd met years ago. A mutual friend named Opal who worked in the entertainment industry had set us up. Opal just said she thought I'd like Ena. And she was right. I'd seen Ena years before in the television series *It*

Takes a Thief, where she played Robert Wagner's secretary. Very sexy woman. Dark chocolate skin and a body that would make you pass out before you got a chance to touch it. I flew Ena out from Hollywood to New York City for the weekend. We stayed at The Plaza and I showed her a good time. We dated off and on for a while, nothing too serious. We lost touch after I got married. And now there she was, looking as beautiful as the last time I'd seen her.

"Miss Hartmann, what brings you to Vegas?"

Ena sat down at the one empty chair that wasn't turned up on the table.

"I'm your good-luck charm, Frank."

She crossed those legs and made sure I could see everything she was working with. Good Lord.

"Excuse me, miss, if you're not playing, I'm going to have to ask you not to sit there," the dealer said.

"Oops, I'm sorry," Ena said. "I'll just stand right here."

Ena stood very close to me. And then she leaned over and put her head on my shoulder. Before I even realized what she was doing, I heard a woman screaming at me from a hundred feet away.

"Fraaaaaaaaaaaaaaaaaaaaaaaaaaaannnnnnnnnnk!"

I jumped and turned around and saw Julie barreling toward me.

"Is that what you came down here to do! Talk to these girls and do God only knows what else!"

"Julie, I don't even know this girl!" I lied.

"Liar!"

Julie grabbed my arm and managed to twist me away from the table. Now, my wife was a bitty little thing. I could have just tossed her aside. But I knew she was mad. And I

was just going to have to try to calm her down. She dragged
me off the casino floor and onto the private elevator that led
us to our suites.

"I can't believe you! You said you were going down to
gamble. But they cleared the floor for you and that . . . that
woman!"

"Not true, Julie Lucas," I said. "Not true at all. You got it
all wrong."

"No. *You* got it all wrong, mister!"

Julie jabbed her finger into my face and then put both
her hands on her hips and glared at me. I almost wanted to
laugh. But I knew that would just piss her off even more.

"Julie," I said, as we went into our main suite. "You're
going to wake the kids up."

"I sent them over to my parents' suite because I wanted
to come down and say hello to you. You big liar!"

I slumped on the couch in the living room and tried to
wait out Julie's tantrum.

"You don't think I know about the women, Frank?"

"What women?"

"All of the goddamn women!"

"I don't know what you heard."

"I'm hearing everything. This one is saying she has your
baby. That one is saying she's your woman. I see a picture of
you with this one. I hear about you at the nightclub with
this one. I am *sick* of this shit."

I rolled my eyes.

"Oh. You don't care?"

Julie picked up a table lamp on the side of the sofa. She
lifted it above her head and threw it right at me. I ducked
and it hit the wall right behind me.

"Julie Lucas!" I said. "I'm gonna have to pay for that!"

"Oh yeah? What about this?" she yelled, picking up the matching lamp on the other side of the sofa. I jumped up to grab her arm but she threw it before I could reach her and it crashed on the wall.

"You gotta pay for this one, too?"

BAM. She threw another lamp.

"And what about this one?"

She took a standing lamp and smashed it into the floor right at her feet.

"Julie, let me talk to you for a second."

But my wife had no words for me. Within ten minutes, no less than ten lamps throughout the suite had been smashed up, stomped on, and thrown against the wall. And I didn't move a muscle. I let her curse me out good and thoroughly. And when she was done, she went over to her parents' suite for the night. I got ready for bed, stepping over all the broken glass and crushed light bulbs. I called the front desk and had them send someone up to give me a tally on how much all the damage would cost. The total was four thousand dollars. I couldn't believe it. That damn wife of mine cost me four thousand dollars. On some damn lamps.

The next morning, Joe came over to take us out for breakfast. The mess had all been cleaned up and it looked like nothing had happened at all. And Julie was just as sweet as ever.

"Good morning, Joe," she said, bringing him in for a kiss on the cheek. She ignored me and continued getting herself and the kids ready.

"I heard there was a bit of a commotion here last night," Joe said.

"Yeah, just a bit."

"Four thousand dollars' worth of trouble," Joe said with a smile.

"Yup," I said, staring at Julie and shaking my head.

Joe stood next to me and held up my hand. "In this corner! Weighing in at two hundred pounds. From La Grange, North Carolina, by way of Harlem USA, it's *Fraaaaaank LuuuuuuCAS!*"

Joe went over to the other end of the suite and took Julie by the hand. "And in this corner! From San Juan, Puerto Rico, weighing one hundred and five pounds, Juuuuuulie Luuuuuuucas!"

Julie smiled and then laughed out loud. "Joe, don't try to make me laugh. I am very upset with Frank."

Joe walked her over to me and put her hand in mine.

"You know this man is crazy about you."

"One of us is crazy, that's for sure," I said.

We never did make it to Hawaii. After Julie's tantrum, I wasn't in the mood for any more traveling. We went right on back to New York. Julie's parents stayed with us for a while and then went back to Puerto Rico. I spent the rest of the time that I was supposed to be vacationing at work instead. I had shipments to oversee and I checked in with Doc Holliday about the daily operations.

"A few of your brothers came by to see me while you were away," said Doc.

"Came to see you for what?"

"Looking for some product," Doc said.

"I told all of them they don't have no business whatsoever in my line of work. Damn."

"Well, seems like they waited until you were out of town for a reason."

"You didn't give them any work, did you?"

"Of course not," Doc said. "I wouldn't do that without talking to you. Especially since they wanted a family discount."

"I'll bet they did."

"You might not be able to keep them out of the game for too long," Doc said. "I turned them down. But someone else might not."

I talked to all my brothers over the next few weeks and tried to explain to them why I didn't want them involved.

"Y'all ain't like me," I told Shorty. "This business is cutthroat. It takes something."

"What makes you think we ain't got it?" Shorty said.

"Look. Maybe you do. I don't want to find out. What do you need? You want to open a business, I'll help you."

"We want in," said Shorty. "That's all the help we want from you."

"I done already told you. The answer is no."

"Then we'll do it without you."

I heard through the grapevine that a few of my brothers approached some of my lower-level lieutenants and finally got enough of a supply to start dabbling in hustling. There was nothing I could do to stop them. Contrary to what's been written about me, I did not want my brothers to go into the drug game.

In *New York Magazine*, a reporter quoted me as saying I wanted to work with "country boys," and that is true. I always kept southern folks close to my operation. Because I'm from the South, I know how we deal with certain situations. A lot of the people I worked with had the same southern roots. I didn't say anything about hiring my own brothers. Though the article made it seem as if I wanted them to work for me, I wish they never had. I can't say this enough.

You have to understand, I was the oldest son. I wanted to protect them from that life. I wanted them to just enjoy what I was able to provide. And furthermore, I was on my way out of the game. I was stacking my money and carefully plotting my exit strategy. As soon as I bought my private plane, I was out of the business. And I wanted to set my brothers up in legal enterprises. It was not the time for them to be just starting out in a business I was almost ready to leave. Almost.

I wanted to give them whatever money they needed. But I should have known that wouldn't work. They were men. They didn't want handouts. Just like I didn't want to just work for Bumpy in a numbers spot for the rest of my life.

I worried about my brothers. My business was kill or be killed. You gotta be Johnny-on-the-spot and handle problems that can get ugly. If you can't handle some real ugly stuff, you'd be better off putting on your wife's apron and staying home. I didn't want them to have any parts of it. I was starting to grow weary of it all myself.

I'd taken my brother Shorty out to Thailand with me once. I was doing a deal, but I'd taken him along just so he could see the country and have a bit of a vacation. My brothers couldn't be satisfied with just allowing me to help them. They didn't want money to buy a house or to tag along on trips. They wanted to make a name for themselves. It was bad timing. I was trying to clean my name up and retire it.

My brothers did get into the game. And they eventually made their way back to Doc, trying to get some of my stuff to sell. I sighed heavily when Doc told me that they were in the game and there was no stopping them.

"Don't charge 'em heavy," I told Doc. "Give 'em the cheapest price we can."

19

"Good morning, Phil Kronfeld's menswear. How can I help you?"

"This is Frank Lucas. Let me speak to Mike Green."

"Speaking. What can I do for you, Mr. Lucas?"

"I heard you got some new material in."

"Just got in a really nice wool blend from Merino, Italy."

"How many different colors?"

"Ten."

"I need twenty suits. Two in each color. Send 'em to the house."

"Which house, sir? Teaneck?"

"Send five to each address."

"Yes, sir."

I was too restless and paranoid to stay in any one place for more than a few nights in a row. I was still on the run from Babyface, who found me way too often for my tastes.

Even after I bought the house in Teaneck, I kept an apartment at the Regency and at the Essex House and had a few other apartments sprinkled around the city.

I was truly a rolling stone in a lot of ways. Wherever I laid my hat was my home. I had a full wardrobe at each place. I really liked my place at 3333 Henry Hudson Parkway. Beautiful building, indoor heated pool, attentive staff. Very upscale neighborhood. And very upper-class neighbors. As far as the people in that building were concerned, I was a wealthy businessman with a housewife and a young daughter. I left the house in the finest suits and drove new, shiny cars and exchanged no more and no less than good morning to the white businessmen I encountered in the underground parking garage. I liked that the building was low-key and not too flashy. Drawing attention to myself had never been my style.

In the early years of my marriage to Julie, before we bought the house in Teaneck, we lived together at the place on Henry Hudson Parkway. As far as I knew, there was only one other drug dealer in the building, a man who lived on the first floor with his wife. Women talk. And the wife ended up telling Julie what her husband did for a living. But the man was quiet and kept to himself, so I didn't mind.

Julie and I had a typical family lifestyle. But because I was in the streets, it was like I lived two separate lives. I'd lived three lifetimes before I even met her. I'd had the twins, down in North Carolina. And then I'd had little Yogi and Frankie Jr., too.

Right before I'd married Julie, I had another child, a baby girl named Candace. Candace's mother was a woman from Alabama named Sarah. She was a pretty little country girl and had just come up north for work. Sarah was young.

And she was still a virgin. She met me and the rest was history. She had my daughter Candace and they lived uptown, over on 123rd Street between 7th and Lenox. I checked in with Sarah and my daughter Candace whenever I could to make sure they had everything they could possibly need.

After Julie and I moved out to Teaneck, I kept the place at 3333 Henry Hudson Parkway as one of my side spots if I needed to be in the city late at night to check on one of my kids or take care of business. One night, I was in the parking garage, getting in my Cadillac to go visit my daughter Candace, when I heard a voice calling out my name. I looked around. No one in that building knew me by name. And if they did, they would be calling me Mr. Lucas.

Who do I see walking toward me but Nicky Barnes. I rolled my eyes.

"Fucking Nicky Barnes. What the hell are you doing here?" I said. "Nicky, please don't tell me you live here."

"Been here for a month. How's it going, Frank?" He grinned at me like he was a mouse who just spotted some cheese.

"Hey, Nicky," I said.

I'm not spending much time on Nicky Barnes in this book. I'll tell you the bare-bones basics of what you need to know. I was Frank Lucas. He was not. Nicky was a drug dealer. I was a supplier. Nicky was a common criminal. I was an entrepreneur who dabbled in illegal enterprises. Nicky was a junkie. I never touched the stuff.

I crossed paths with Nicky here and there, mostly on the social scene. But the way Nicky operated was very distasteful to me. He was always being photographed, always talking to reporters. He was in shootouts with the cops in broad daylight, speeding through New York City like something out of a movie. He brought way too much attention to the underworld. And plus, I just didn't like him. Too loud and too excitable. I didn't get down with him at all. And I was pissed off when I saw him in that parking garage.

"Nice building, right, Frank? I like it a lot."

"Is that so?"

"Frank, you said we could talk about you joining The Council."

Nicky had been on me for years to join some kind of organization with him and a few other dealers. The very idea of that was a joke to me. None of them were on my level. I worked alone, headed up my own shit. And I didn't want anything to do with the rest of them.

"Let's talk about it right now," I said. "I'm not joining shit."

"We need to protect ourselves, Frank. It's getting crazy out there."

"And you think I need your protection?"

"I just think we'd make more money if we divided the city up. You could have—"

"Are you out of your mind? Divide the city up for what? What would that do for me? You try selling your weak shit anywhere near me and you know you'll be flat broke. The whole city is mine. And I don't share."

"Just think about it. Don't have to decide right now."

"Anything else, Nicky?"

"Need you to front me a few keys. I'm short this month. You know I'm good for it."

I opened the door to my car and climbed in.

"Fine. Call Doc."

"Thanks, Frank," Nicky said, as I started to close the door. "Guess I'll be seeing you all the time now!"

"Imagine that," I said, before starting the car and peeling out of the garage on two wheels.

I never went back to the apartment at 3333 Henry Hudson Parkway again. Didn't get any of my clothes or other personal effects. I wasn't trying to be within one hundred feet of Nicky Barnes. Especially not at my home. No idea what happened to that apartment. I'd paid my rent in full and in advance for about a year. But that didn't matter to me one bit. I had to be comfortable wherever I lived. And if Nicky wanted to live there, he could have that building all to himself.

20

October 26, 1970. That's when my trouble really started. I went down to Atlanta to watch Muhammad Ali's return to boxing. After three years of having his boxing license revoked for refusing to enlist in the draft, he was fighting this guy named Jerry Quarry. Jerry was known as a bleeder. He couldn't take no kind of punch without getting cut up. I go down to Atlanta to see this fight and I don't pay no mind to how I'm dressed or any of that shit. I'm clean, of course. But not flashy. We just went down to see Ali fight and have a good time. Wasn't trying to impress nobody.

Well, I get to Atlanta and dealers from California are in town for the fight, too. And some of these cats are wearing mink coats. Now, it's October. In Atlanta. Hot as shit. And these motherfuckers are wearing mink coats and hats—all kinds of extravagant shit. I couldn't believe it. And they're looking me up and down and saying all kinds of slick shit, like I'm crazy for wearing something regular.

"We thought you was big time up in New York City," said one guy from L.A.

"Yeah, I heard them niggas up in New York always had on the fly shit," said another guy standing with him.

"It's a boxing match," I said. "Not a fashion show."

The fight was sold out and I spent the whole night hearing these gangsters from L.A. and down South strutting around the place, acting like they were the shit 'cause they spent a little money on a mink coat. I knew right then and there I was going to take care of them.

The fight was held in the Atlanta Auditorium, right downtown. Ali beat Quarry, like everyone knew he would, and the celebration spilled out into the streets of Atlanta after it was over. Nothing but people talking shit, laughing, and having a good time.

I told everybody down there to bring their asses to New York City for the next fight and I would show them all that we knew how to get down in New York. I wasn't prepared for people trying to look all high-class at a boxing match. But if that's how they wanted to get down—I would show 'em. And I screamed it out to whoever would listen:

"Y'all think you gone outshine me? Bring that ass to New York City and I will show every last one of y'all who the boss is. Bring it to New York City! You will see. As sure as my name is Frank Lucas!"

That's the thing. My name is Frank Lucas. And there is no such thing as outtalking me, outhustling me, outthinking me, or outdressing me. Might be able to get away with some of that stuff today. But in 1970? No. I wasn't letting it happen. Under any circumstances.

So I fly back to New York City after the fight and I already have a plan. The next time a major fight came to New York City, I was gonna make those flashy motherfuckers from California and Atlanta wish they had never challenged me.

It was soon announced that Ali was going to fight Joe Frazier at Madison Square Garden on March 8, 1971. I smiled to myself as I watched the announcement on the news. And the next morning I had one of my assistants make me an appointment with Joseph and Ron, two furriers who owned a shop in midtown.

"I need something different. Something unique," I explained to Joseph. We sat in the office in the rear of their showroom, surrounded by different pelts and fabrics.

"We can make you a floor-length mink coat, Mr. Lucas," said Ron, showing me a piece of mink fabric.

"I don't want no fucking mink," I spat. "Everybody and their mother has a mink coat. I said I want something unique. Something no one has ever seen before."

Joseph and Ron exchanged a glance. "What about this, Mr. Lucas. It's Russian sable, very beautiful."

I touched the pelt and then put it aside.

"It looks too much like mink." I sat back and looked around the showroom. "Y'all ain't got nothing really different? Come on now."

"Do you like chinchilla?"

"Chinchilla," I repeated. "What the hell is that?"

Joseph went across the room and returned with a sample. The fur was thick and fluffy, gray with black streaks. I'd never see anything like it before in my life.

"That's it right there," I said, standing up to leave. "I want a maxi-length coat with this right here." I stopped to look at my reflection in the mirror. "And a hat, too."

"Wait, Mr. Lucas," said Ron, trying to keep up with me as I walked toward the exit. "This would be much too expensive for an entire coat. Maybe we can just use it to trim a wool coat?"

"Make it. I don't care how much it costs," I said. "You need a deposit?"

"Yes, sir. But you don't understand. To make a coat out of this, it would be—"

I rolled my eyes and took out my checkbook. "How much do you need right now?"

"We . . . we . . . we'd need about half, sir. But that—"

"How much is it gonna cost me?"

Ron closed his eyes and made a face like he was scared that I was going to hit him. "The coat will be one hundred thousand dollars, sir. And the hat will be twenty-five thousand."

I scribbled out a check and put it on the table. "Here's sixty thousand. Call my assistant when you're ready for a fitting."

It was six weeks until the fight at Madison Square Garden and I heard through various friends that just about everyone who had come out to the fight in Atlanta would be in New York for the Ali–Frazier fight. This was not going to be just any sporting event. This was the biggest thing New York City had seen in a hundred years. Two of the best fighters—in their prime—duking it out for the heavyweight championship of the world.

I knew I was going to have to represent. For myself and for Harlem, my adopted hometown.

I went down to the showroom for three or four fittings to get my coat looking just right. They had to resize that hat a few times. I've got a big head and they just couldn't get the pattern right. In the meantime, I had a suit made. Could have gotten a suit off the rack, but fuck that. I wanted it all custom, from the suit to the shoes. I paid a few thousand for the suit and another thousand for the shoes.

Just a week or two before the fight I went down to the showroom for the final fitting. I slipped into the coat and adjusted the hat on my head and took in my reflection in the full-length mirror. All I could do was let out a low whistle and make a 360-degree turn. My shit was hot. There was no denying that. No one going to that fight was ready for me.

Picture it. I'm forty-four years old and in my prime. I wasn't no pretty boy. But not ugly, either. I'm standing there, over six feet tall, just over two hundred pounds. Caramel-brown skin, just like my daddy, with an easy, wide grin.

When I stepped out of my limousine that night, right on Eighth Avenue, at the entrance to Madison Square Garden, the crowd screamed like I was a rock star. And not a soul gathered knew who the hell I was. All they knew was that a black man came out there rocking a maxi-length chinchilla looking like a million bucks and that was enough for them. I came to the fight alone; my wife, Julie, had recently suffered a miscarriage and had gone to her native Puerto Rico to spend time with her family and recover. As soon as I got out of the car, this sexy young thing with big brown eyes sidled up next to me.

"I love what you're wearing, sir," she said. "Can I take a picture with you?"

"You don't even know me," I said, sizing up her legs.

"I don't need to know you," she said. "I just know I want to take a picture with you."

She stood next to me and somewhere a camera flashed and I continued on my way into the arena. And man, them fools I had seen down in Atlanta? Their faces were tight. They knew they couldn't fuck with me!

I saw one guy I'd seen in Atlanta, standing with some woman who looked as broke-down as he did. He was wearing the same mink coat he'd worn in Atlanta.

"Good to see you," I said. His woman looked me up and down and then looked away. I saw several of the men I'd seen in Atlanta and they were all staring at me in disbelief.

Some of them refused to even come into the arena! I heard from my people that a few of them didn't even come to the fight after they saw how I was doing it. Heard they just turned around and went back to their hotels. Didn't even come to the fight! Who the hell wants to come in there when I'm looking like I own New York City?

Them fools was making a million dollars a year, if they were lucky, selling dope in Los Angeles and Atlanta. I was Frank Lucas—clearing that in a day, easy. And for the first time ever, I actually felt like showing off. It was not my style. Up until that point, I was fine with being the Haint of Harlem, a faceless name that most people on the street could not identify. But just one time, I wanted to put people on notice. I wanted to be seen. And I wanted people to know that I was on top of the world in every single way. I could not have people who made less money than me walking around thinking they ruled the world.

The Ali–Frazier fight separated the boys from the men. Anybody who was half of somebody was there. Frank Sinatra was there. He couldn't get ringside seats, so he was in the press section, taking pictures for *Life* magazine. Frank

Sinatra himself! Superstars like Diana Ross, Barbra Streisand, and Dustin Hoffman tried to sit in the press area since they couldn't get ringside seats, either. They ended up getting chased out of there and forced to sit elsewhere. It was a night to end all nights. One for the history books. And I was there, front and center, soaking in the electricity of it all.

When I say I was there front and center, I mean it. On a night when even the vice president of the United States of America was forced to sit in the balcony, Frank Lucas was close enough to spit in the ring.

Before Ali and Frazier entered the arena, I saw a lot of my people taking their seats and greeting one another. Joe Louis came down the aisle and stopped to give me a big hug before he made his way to his seat. Ali came down and also gave me a hug before going into the ring. And then here comes Joe Frazier, heading into the ring: he winks at me on his way into his corner.

"You better not get no blood on my fucking coat!" I yelled out to Frazier.

Frazier just laughed as he continued jogging and shadowboxing down to the ring.

And then, just before the fight began, I saw Frank Matthews, sitting in my row, just a few seats down from where I sat.

Frank "Pee Wee" Matthews was a well-known heroin dealer in Harlem at the time. We were colleagues, you could say. And I had a lot of respect for him. I can't say we were close friends, but we definitely were friendly and liked to razz each other good-naturedly when we crossed paths. Frank was from North Carolina, too, so we had that in common. We were both country boys who came up to New York City to do big things.

Pee Wee was a flashy motherfucker. Always with the mink coats and the bright-colored suits. He pulled up to the fight that night in a chauffer-driven Rolls-Royce. So we were going back and forth, teasing each other about who was really the man that night.

Pee Wee leaned over in his seat (there were two or three guys between us) and yelled over to me.

"So, Frank," he said, nodding his head toward the ring. "What you want to do?"

"You call it," I said, smiling right back at him.

"A hunnid," he said.

"Damn motherfucker! Why you so cheap tonight!" I said with a laugh.

"How about two?"

I rolled my eyes and didn't even bother turning in his direction. "Please. I'm insulted. What about four?"

"Let's make it five then," he said.

"Done deal," I said, smiling.

I didn't know then that the three men sitting between us were federal agents with the DEA. And here are me and Pee Wee, dressed in a million dollars' worth of finery between us. And betting a half million on the fight.

What started in Atlanta at the Ali–Quarry fight had now reached the point of no return. I'd made a massive mistake—one I'm still paying for today. I was so busy trying to outshine other folks with material goods that I started slipping. It's a quality I'd observed in others—and sworn to myself that I would avoid. It just wasn't my style or my nature to be gaudy and flashy. But every man has weaknesses, temptations. And just once, I'd decided to go outside my character. But it only takes once, as I would soon learn. And by the time Frazier was declared the winner, I'd been transformed. I came to the fight an unknown man—at least as far as the DEA was concerned.

I left that fight a marked man.

21

"Frank, where do you get all this from?"

My mother was looking me dead in my eye as I nursed a drink in my living room at the Teaneck house.

"All what?" I asked, keeping my eyes on the television.

My mother stood in front of the television to block my view.

"Color television, fancy cars. God only knows how many fancy clothes and shoes you and Julie have."

"Momma, I'm doing well for myself. I have a lot of different—"

"A lot of different what?" my mother said, her hands on her hips.

"Different business ventures," I said, standing up.

"Frank Lucas, I want to know exactly where you're getting this money from. And I want to know right now."

I sighed heavily and took my mother's hand in mine. "No, Momma, you don't," I said.

I kissed her hand and left the room. She didn't follow me.

A few weeks after that conversation, I knew Johnny Law was getting close. Can't tell you how I knew. I just knew. You can't run a business like I did and not just have a feeling about it.

For starters, Frank "Pee Wee" Matthews had disappeared.

After the Ali–Frazier fight, it was back to business as usual for me. But things had started getting hectic for Pee Wee. The cops were all over him, busting his people and getting closer to a major indictment for him. I kept up with his case through the news. I had to know what was going on with him so that I could be sure to avoid his fate.

In the summer of 1973, the feds finally got him on a major indictment. His bail was set at a couple hundred thousand. He posted bail and was supposed to appear in court a few weeks later.

No one has ever seen Frank "Pee Wee" Matthews since. He just disappeared. Vanished into thin air. From what I heard on the streets at the time, he had at least twenty million dollars. That's enough to disappear for a good long time. Now, some people say he must have been killed. That he couldn't disappear for so long without getting caught. I happen to think Frank's still alive, living somewhere in Africa, laughing at the feds still trying to catch him.

But at the time, when Frank first disappeared, it marked a change in the streets. All the major dealers at the time, including me, knew that Frank's disappearance was going to make things tight for all of us. The feds were going to start cracking down. They were going to have to take someone down. If they couldn't get us off the street, they wouldn't be able to justify their salaries. So I knew I would have to tighten my operations and make sure everything was under the radar. Or at least as under the radar as I could make it.

To make matters even worse, it was around this time that I got even more unsettling news: Melvin Combs had been killed. Melvin was the flashy but good-hearted guy that I'd been cool with for years. He'd gotten caught up in an indictment with Willie Abraham and his people. Willie was a big-time dealer who was also being watched by the feds. They brought him down and Melvin was shot and killed before the case went to trial. I heard rumors that people thought Melvin had given information to the cops. But I know that wasn't true. I just know it. That wasn't Melvin's style. And anyone who says different is lying. Melvin's death hit me hard. And I went even deeper into a shell.

Unfortunately, ever since the night me and Pee Wee made that bet at the Ali–Frazier fight, the feds had their eyes on me, and though I made it my business to stay underground, there were still eyes everywhere, watching my every move.

And then, just a few months after Pee Wee disappeared and Melvin was killed, Zack Robinson vanished.

Ever since that day he checked on me at Bumpy's funeral, Zack and I had always kept in touch. We'd been through a lot together. We opened Lloyd Price's Turntable together and we'd both invested in that movie *The Rip Off*. So I was concerned when the streets were whispering that he was gone.

Zack got hit with an indictment and I heard through the streets that he was planning to jump bail and make a run for it, just like Pee Wee. But from what I hear, it didn't work out like he'd planned. Someone told me that his lawyers, who were supposed to be helping him skip town, told him to bring all the money he had to a burger joint on Eighty-sixth

Street and Third Avenue. Had to be close to fifty million dollars. Word was that they shot and killed Zack, put weights on him, and threw him into the Atlantic.

If that is the way it went down, I don't know why Zack would bring all his money with him and trust anyone to get him out of town. If it had been me, I would have said, I'll bring a million, that's all I've got. And then make sure someone else had access to the rest of my money and could get it to me if I needed it.

I guess Zack just wasn't thinking clearly.

Hearing about what happened to Zack left a real bad taste in my mouth. Either people were getting locked up or they were skipping bail and disappearing or ending up dead. And I knew that the heat was close to me, too.

Babyface was still on the scene, showing up at one of my homes whenever he could catch me and shaking me down for more and more money. I didn't care about the money. It was still pouring in from the streets. I rarely had to travel overseas anymore. I had a fine-tuned operation from Southeast Asia to Harlem. My lieutenants were still handing over millions of dollars in tens and twenties to me. I'd squirrel them away in different spots until it was time for my associates to take another flight to the Cayman Islands. Only on the rarest occasions did I take the money to my house in Teaneck. And if I did have to take it there, it never stayed in the house for more than twenty-four hours.

But anytime I did it, I thought about Bumpy Johnson. I could see his face so clearly. When I first started working with him, he looked me in the eye and told me: "Leave that life out there. When you cross that threshold of your home, don't bring any of that into your home. Ever."

He said it to me more than once. And thirty years later, I wasn't following that advice. I knew that was a bad move. Even though I'd stayed one step ahead for a very long time, that kind of luck never lasts.

On a cold winter's night in January 1975, I brought home about eight million dollars. It was all in the trunk of my Cadillac. Before I brought anything into the house, I came inside first. And as soon as my daughter, Francine, heard the key in the door, she came running to the front hallway.

"Daddy! I missed you!"

I held my little girl close and kissed her on the cheek. "Daddy missed you, too. Have you been a good girl?"

Francine shook her head solemnly. "Nope."

I laughed and let Francine tell me all about her day. Julie was there, on the phone with one of her parents in Puerto Rico. Our full-time housekeeper was finishing the last of her responsibilities. When she was gone, I put Francine to bed, talked to my wife for a few minutes, and then I went out to get the money, bundled into luggage, and brought it up to the attic.

Julie was in bed, watching television, and she saw me heading up to the attic.

"I thought you said no more keeping money here, Frank. You promised."

"Last time, Julie Lucas," I said with a heavy sigh. "Very last time."

"Always the last time," Julie said. "Every time is the last time."

The next morning, one of my associates and my brother Shorty were flying down to the Cayman Islands with my latest batch of cash. I had eleven million dollars in total in my attic. They were scheduled to come to the house and pick it up before heading straight to the airport. I hated having large amounts of money in the house. But sometimes it had to be done for just a short bit of time. I slept like a rock that night.

"This fucking money! Nothing but trouble! We never needed it. Don't care about the money. You want it? Take it. Take all of the *goddamn* money!"

My wife, Julie, had lost it. Law enforcement agents had swarmed our house on the morning of January 28, 1975. I was surrounded by agents on all sides in the living room. They were asking me where the money was. I didn't say a word. They didn't even have a goddamn search warrant. A few agents went upstairs to talk to Julie. I had hoped that she'd be able to keep her cool when they started needling her. But that had never been Julie's style. I don't know what they said to her. But the next thing I know, I could hear her screaming. As I stood on the first floor, singles and five-dollar bills began to rain down from the second floor onto the front yard. I shook my head.

"Looks like your wife knows where the money is," said one agent.

"All I know is, until I see a search warrant, you better not touch anything in my house," I said.

"We're working on that," said another officer. "Meanwhile, don't move a fucking muscle."

An officer led my son Yogi and my daughter, Francine, out of the house, where a family member was waiting to take them away from the scene. I caught a glimpse of both of them, silent but in tears, and it broke my fucking heart.

Let me get something straight right now. These cops weren't just trying to bust me to send me to jail for being a big, bad drug dealer. Hell no. They knew what kind of money I was working with. And they wanted it. I knew for a fact that they could have come with a search warrant right away. They wanted to see what they could find on their own before they started any kind of "official" search.

"I didn't see anything in the bedrooms," said a young officer. "Just a couple thousand in a dresser."

"Doing a lot of searching for someone with no search warrant," I said.

"We're already arresting your wife for obstruction of justice, so I suggest you keep your mouth shut."

"You gotta be fucking kidding me," I said. "Just because she threw some money out of a window?"

For three hours, they kept us in the house. I wasn't allowed to get in touch with my attorney and I wasn't officially arrested or charged with any crime. They finally got their search warrant and tore that house apart. They were peeling back wallpaper, breaking open furniture. They destroyed that house.

I was finally arrested and charged with conspiracy to distribute heroin. They arrested Julie for obstruction of justice. They knew full well that my wife had nothing to do with my operation. They just did that to fuck with me. I was taken down to Fifty-seventh Street for processing and then to West Street to wait for a bail hearing. I called a lawyer I'll call Jeff Hoffman.

"Am I gonna get bail?" I asked him.

"I'll make sure of it."

"What are we looking like, Jeff?"

"Not good, Frank."

"Did they find the money?"

"They said they found a half million, most of which was the money that Julie threw out of the window."

"That was just chump change. Did they find the real money? The money you were supposed to take to the islands."

"I don't think so. They had a press conference. They're just saying they found a little over four hundred thousand."

"Find my money."

"I will, Frank," he said. "I already sent your brother over to check it out."

I had been arrested before. But I knew this time was different. I didn't know how much they knew about my operations and how deep in the game I was. I wasn't worried, though. Not even a little bit. All I wanted to know was where my money was. The next day, when my attorney came to see me, I got my answer.

"It's gone, Frank. All of it."

"You better be fucking kidding me."

"I'm not. They stole it. The money in the attic is gone. I called the prosecutor to ask him again how much money they found. He said the cops reported five hundred and eighty-five thousand dollars. They stole the fucking money, Frank."

"Those motherfuckers."

"It gets worse."

"It better not."

"They found the safe-deposit key. For the box on the Cayman Islands. They don't know what it goes to. But it's in the evidence room, and they're trying to figure it out."

"Well, you better get your ass on a plane and get my shit before then."

"I'm leaving in an hour."

But my lawyer was too late. By the time he got to the safe-deposit box, someone had been down there and cleaned me out.

I stood before a judge the next day to plead. I yelled out *not guilty* as clear as a bell. If the cops who stole the money from me were still on the force, spending my money like it was going out of style, then I damn sure wasn't guilty of a goddamn thing.

I got out on bail and immediately got to work handling my business. I had to make sure things would still run smoothly whether I got locked up or not. My lieutenants were in place, handling shipments coming in and making sure the money was still flowing. Julie was released on bail as well and I tried to comfort her. But I really wasn't sure what would happen at her trial. Francine was still with relatives. But Yogi, who was fifteen, needed even more stability. I wanted him to stay in school and get ready for college. And I wasn't sure what would happen with me. I talked to my good friend Joe Louis and his wife, Martha. They agreed to take Yogi and have him go to school out in Vegas to prepare for college.

I still had good sums of money in other places throughout the country. And I also owned a nice amount of real estate. So it wasn't like I was broke as I waited for the trial to start.

I was facing two separate trials: the feds charged me with conspiracy, along with a few other drug dealers, and the state charged me with distributing heroin.

Whatever would happen would happen. I was ready either way. And I didn't intend on my legal trouble affecting my business one iota.

22

The chief witness in the conspiracy case was some guy named Charles Morris, supposedly a narcotics dealer. My attorneys made mincemeat out of that witness. Made him look like a lying fool in front of that jury. He couldn't keep his stories straight and could barely even remember the names of all the people he was supposedly working for. Looking back, I think he was trying to help me out. I think he changed his mind about testifying at the last minute.

The trial lasted for a few weeks. And my friend Joe Louis, who had flown out to pick up my son Yogi, came to every single day of the trial, after his wife, Martha, had flown Yogi back out to their home in Las Vegas.

My parents were also there every single day, which made me upset. I told them both to stay away. I didn't want them hearing all the stuff that was going on at the trial, and I'd always gone out of my way to keep them far removed from my criminal life. But they both insisted on showing their support and there was nothing I could do about it but accept it.

Right around Christmas, we got the verdict. We were acquitted. All of us. On all charges. I was a free man. I'd been pretty confident that they didn't have enough evidence to make the verdict stick. They were trying to tie me together with a whole bunch of dealers in a way that just didn't make sense. I only dealt with other dealers when I absolutely had to, which wasn't very often, so it would have been impossible to prove that I had some kind of conspiracy across the board with a bunch of other criminals.

I had one trial over and done with. But I immediately had to stand trial in the state case I faced for heroin distribution. And, as I suspected, I was found guilty. At the sentencing a few weeks later, I was given forty years in prison and fined two hundred thousand dollars.

And none of it bothered me a single bit. I had enough money in the streets and enough trusted people out there. My cell became my new headquarters. It was business as usual.

I was sent to the Trenton State Prison in New Jersey. And I swear, I had that place running like I fucking owned it. I poured money into that place, from the guards to the cooks and everyone in between.

"You got a delivery today, Lucas," said Jack, one of the guards. "Ten T-bone steaks, a few porterhouses."

"Let me get a T-bone steak, cook it medium," I said, not taking my head away from the newspaper I was reading.

"I think they may have some baked potatoes in there. You want me to tell them that you want that, too?"

"Yeah. And some broccoli. Thanks, Jack."

"No problem."

I was still friendly with Billie Mays. And when I got locked up, she would bring me care packages every week. We weren't allowed to receive raw food, so she would buy steaks and other cuts of meat, cook them just enough so that they weren't raw, and then package them individually and send them to the prison. I had my own section in the prison kitchen just for my food. I'm telling you—I ate better in that jail than most of those wardens ate at home. And I would bet any amount of money on that.

I never went into the mess hall at Trenton State. There was no need. I ordered every meal like it was room service at the Regency and had it sent directly to my cell. None of the food they made for the prisoners ever touched my lips. I had fresh fish, grilled to perfection, with garden salads and baked potatoes. I had steaks, macaroni and cheese . . . whatever I had a taste for.

There were a few people I was friendly with. I was even cool with Rubin "Hurricane" Carter. Funny, we'd both end up having our life stories played by the same man years later. I would never have believed that back then.

I made sure all my people ate good, too. I'd send word to the cook to send steak, lobster, squab, or whatever I was having that night to the cells of my friends.

Every prisoner was supposed to have a job. I worked when I wanted to, usually in the library or on the prison newspaper. But I never went if I didn't want to.

Julie was still out on bail from her charges and waiting to stand trial for obstruction of justice. In the meantime, she came down every weekend with Francine.

One weekend, I got called down for a visit. I assumed it was Julie and Francine, though it was a bit earlier than she usually arrived. It was a window visit, which meant I would go to an assigned spot and sit across a window with my visitor.

"You have a Billie Mays here to see you," the guard said. "Go to window number eleven and wait."

I made my way down to the window. But when I sat down, I didn't see Billie. I looked out into the room where the visitors came in and I could just see a whole mess of guards trying to break up some kind of disturbance.

"Two women fighting out there," a guard told me.

As soon as he said that, I looked out and saw little Francine dashing into the room. She stopped at the first window and jumped up to look inside.

"Daddy, are you in there?" I heard her say.

Then she ran to the next window and jumped up to look in. I ducked down. I put two and two together real quick. Julie must have come down earlier with Francine, and she and Billie Mays must have crossed paths. I stayed down and snuck out of the room, making sure Francine didn't see me. I was going to have to figure out what the hell was going on out there before I let Francine see me.

"What happened out there?" I asked one of the guards after I made it back to the waiting area.

"Your wife was standing on line to sign in. She just looked over at this lady and said, 'Is your name Billie?' The woman said yes and she just walked over and punched her right in the face."

I put my head in my hands. "Oh Lord."

"Next thing I know, they're rolling around on the floor. That wife of yours is no joke."

"Tell me about it."

"Are you going out there for your visit?"

"Where are they now?"

"You're wife's waiting to see you. The other woman left."

I went back out and there was Julie, holding Francine on her lap. Francine was waving. Julie's face was stone.

"Frank. You had that woman coming here to see you?"

I waved at Francine and blew her a kiss. She caught it dramatically and blew me one back.

"Do you hear me talking to you, Frank? I want to know why you have other women coming here to see you. And I want some answers right now!"

"Look. Don't argue with me in front of the baby," I said. "We can talk about that later."

We never got a chance to talk about it. Soon after that visit, Julie had to stand trial for throwing that money out the window. They said she was trying to hide it. Which was a lie. She'd had a fit and threw it out the window in plain view of the officers. But they just wanted to punish me for getting acquitted, so they sentenced my wife to five years in prison. That was a damn shame. Taking her away from my baby like that. It was flat-out wrong. They knew full well she wasn't trying to hide no money. That right there hurt me something awful. I wasn't no kind of good husband to Julie, but I cared for her in my own way. And she was my family. And right was right. And the way she had been punished just wasn't right.

I was still getting shipments from Southeast Asia to various military bases while I was locked up. That hadn't changed at all. The money was still flowing. And I was still at the top of my game. I wasn't retiring quite yet. And I had no intentions of serving forty years in prison. So I wanted to make sure I had my money together for whenever I got out.

And I was definitely planning to get out.

23

After I'd been locked up for about a year, I was transferred from New Jersey to Manhattan. It was even better for me because it was easier to run things being right in New York City instead of an hour away from all the action.

I got word from one of my lieutenants that I had six million dollars in profits ready to be sent wherever I wanted it to go. It was difficult to talk on the phone with my crew or tell them what I needed during a visit. So I began to use my attorneys more and more to run my business.

One of my attorneys was a man named Gino Gallina.

"Six million," I told him in the waiting room.

Gino nodded, pretending to point out some information in some legal documents.

"I see," he said, showing me the paperwork. "And where do you want it to go."

"Call Doc," I said. "He knows what to do with it."

The next time I heard from Doc, he had some disturbing news.

"Got the delivery. A bit shorter than I expected."

"Shorter? What the fuck are you talking about?"

"Six hundred thousand missing."

"Not for long, I'll tell you that much," I said, hanging up the phone.

I got in touch with Gino and told him to come see me ASAP. He stalled for over a week. And I realized that this fool was trying to fuck with my money. Not a good move on his part. Not a good move at all.

"Can't get down there today, Frank," he said the next time I called. "Maybe next week."

"Next week? Are you crazy?"

"I'm trying to tell you, I'm all the way out on Long Island. Even if I could come today, I couldn't make it there before—"

"LET ME TELL YOU THIS ONE MORE TIME," I screamed. "GET YOUR ASS HERE BEFORE I FUCKING KILL YOU FROM THIS GODDAMN JAIL CELL."

Gallina must have known I was serious, 'cause less than an hour later, he was sitting in front of me in the waiting room.

"Now, Frank, there's no need for you to get all excited. I've been busy trying to take care of business."

"Where's my money, Gino?"

"I don't know what you're talking about."

"The money you picked up."

"Yeah, I delivered it."

"It was short. Where's my money, Gino?"

One of the guards came over to my chair and said, "Mr. Lucas, we're gonna need you to take it down a little bit."

I looked at the guard. He backed up and went right back to the door.

"I'm listening, Gino."

"I had to use some of it to pay off some expenses and then I was going to put it right back. But then I had to pay off the guys who were keeping an eye on Julie and Francine. And then your brother said he needed to—"

"You're bullshitting me, Gino," I said calmly. "Where the fuck is my money?"

"I told you, Frank, I needed to use some of it to—"

"That was a month ago!" I screamed. "Where the fuck is my money now?"

"I told you I don't have it right now, Frank! Now leave it alone. You'll get the rest of your money."

"Are you out of your goddamn mind?" I said.

I rose up from the chair, overturned the table, and made a dash for Gallina's neck. I squeezed my hands around his neck, shaking him.

"You don't know better than to fuck with my money?" I asked, watching his eyes bulge. I kneed him in the stomach, threw him down on the floor, and began stomping him on the head.

"I will fucking kill you if you don't get my money together and I mean now."

The guards didn't even bother to try to break it up.

I got word soon after that visit that Gino had replaced my missing money. Don't know what happened to him after that. I never saw him again. But even though I got my money back, I now had bigger problems. The news about the incident in the visiting room had spread fast. And someone decided to drop dime and tell the feds that I was still running things from the prison.

They supposedly had all kinds of evidence on me and an airtight case. I wasn't sure about that. And I wasn't so sure I couldn't buy my way out of the case anyway. But my lawyer at the time told me that if I pled not guilty and still lost the case, I'd be looking at life in prison. I pled guilty and was convicted on September 19, 1977.

Now I had seven years added onto my original sentence, to be served concurrently.

And I still didn't care. It slowed down my enterprises a bit. But none of my top brass had been taken down. You would think that after that case, I would stop my operations on the outside. I did not. Why should I? How could I? I had to make sure my family would be taken care of. And I still hadn't given up hope that I would get out somehow, get my money and retire. Only dream I'd given up on was the private plane. I didn't want that anymore.

A few months after that case was over, I got a strange visit.

"Attorney general is here to see you," one of the guards said.

"The what?"

"Attorney general, said he needs to talk to you."

I didn't know what that could be about. But it sounded strange to me. I hadn't been in touch with my attorneys all that much at that point. We had been working on appeals, but I knew the attorney general wouldn't have anything to do with that.

I went to the visiting room and waited. A lawyer I knew named Stanley came in with a man I'd never seen before.

"This is Michael Egan, associate U.S. attorney general."

"What can I do for you?" I said, shaking his hand.

"How interested are you in getting out of here?"

I didn't say a word. I just made a face to let him know I was still listening. The lawyer guy started talking.

"He's looking for a payout, Frank. We know you've got money. He'll get you out of here for a million."

I had more than a million socked away. It would be easy to get my hands on a million dollars. Too easy. But were these two for real? How does the U.S. attorney general come down to a prison and offer someone like me a deal to get out of jail for a million dollars in drug money? I knew stranger things had happened. But I couldn't quite understand why it was happening to me. I didn't know the lawyer very well. I think he'd worked as an assistant to other lawyers on one of my many cases. It just all didn't add up.

"Can you get your hands on a million, Frank?" the lawyer asked. "We'll have you out a week later."

I smelled bullshit, but I played along.

"Let's talk about it in a few days."

They both seemed reluctant to end the meeting and wanted me to give them an answer right then and there. That's when I knew they were full of shit. If they were serious, they would have known that it would have taken time. Only an idiot would have agreed to a plan like that right away.

Sure enough, I found out from one of the guards that the attorney general had written down a different name in the visitors' log. That huge mistake tipped off the authorities. Turns out he wasn't the attorney general. He'd cooked up a plan with that lawyer to try to trick me out of a million dollars.

I don't know what happened to either of them but I

know they were both indicted in federal court. I knew right away that they were both tricksters. But I was still concerned that they saw me as a potential mark. Were people on the street talking about how much money I had and how they could get some of it? I was questioning whether or not my wife was safe. My daughter was in Puerto Rico with her grandparents. Was she safe? Would someone cook up some kind of scheme to get money from me using her as a pawn? From within prison, I hired private security to keep tabs on my daughter and other family members. I stayed in touch with my wife to make sure she was not being approached by anyone with any ridiculous schemes, either.

By the time I'd been locked up for over a year, things began to slow down in the business. My brothers had been locked up; things were changing in the streets. It was getting harder and harder to run things. There was a lot of pressure from Johnny Law.

In 1977, I got a visit in prison from Thelma, Nicky Barnes's wife.

"Nicky wanted me to ask you about something," she said.

"What's that?"

"*The New York Times* wants to do a story on him. Put him on the cover and everything. He wanted to ask you if he could do it."

It was standard procedure that any of the top dealers in Harlem would check in with one another if anything was going down that might bring attention to the rest of us.

"Absolutely not!" I said. "That's the dumbest shit I've ever heard."

"Look, Frank, you know how Nicky is. He just wanted to give you a heads-up, out of respect."

"Well, out of respect, tell him there is no way in the world

I will sanction that move. The streets are hot right now and he wants to put himself in a magazine? Hell no."

"I'll give him the message," Thelma said, standing up to leave.

"Yeah, you do that."

Dumbass Nicky Barnes didn't listen to me. This fool voluntarily put himself on the cover of *The New York Times Magazine*, talking about how he was Mr. Untouchable. When I got the paper in prison, I threw it up in the air when I saw his mug staring out from the front cover. What an idiot. I knew things were even tighter after that. Sure enough, they took him down and a whole bunch of other folks. The whole climate and culture of the heroin industry as I'd known it was quickly coming to an end.

I was still dabbling. But it was nothing like it used to be, and I wasn't sure if it ever would be. From behind the prison walls, I heard a lot about other dealers going down. I didn't hear anything about the crooked cops who busted us and stole our money. And that pissed me off. Babyface and some of his crew in the special investigations unit were still on the streets, claiming to help clean up Harlem while making millions and lying through their teeth.

And law enforcement had me locked up and was still trying to get more and more time tacked onto my sentence.

In 1980, I went to trial for allegedly ordering a hit on someone who testified against me in the first case against me in '74. Now, I'm not going to say I didn't have the power to order someone killed. But this man who ended up dead at a block party had nothing to do with me. Nothing whatsoever. But law enforcement was desperate to tie me to anything and everything.

I was acquitted of the crime. As I knew I would be. But

still, in jail I sat. While crooked cops spent my money and looked for more and more ways to keep me locked up.

And it pissed me off royally. I wasn't planning to rot in jail while they lived the high life. Hell no.

24

A few years after I got busted, my brothers were arrested for conspiracy to distribute heroin. While they were out on bail and awaiting trial, I got a visit in prison from a man named Richie Roberts. Roberts was the assistant Essex County prosecutor who was trying to take my brothers down.

People think Richie Roberts arrested me, like he did in the movie. Not true. I never even laid eyes on Richie until that day he came to see me.

"Nice to meet you, Mr. Lucas," Richie said. "Heard lots of nice things about you."

"What do you want?"

"You're going to be indicted in this case, too. I thought you should know that."

"For what?" I asked. "I didn't have anything to do with whatever my brothers were into."

"Maybe not. But I still think you could be valuable for this trial. I need you in that courtroom."

"So even if you know I had nothing to do with them, you want to use me for star power?"

Richie smiled. "Something like that."

"This is ridiculous."

"It's not you I want, Frank," Richie said. "It's your brother Shorty. But if I don't have you in this case, I'll lose it all."

"I just got indicted by the feds for another conspiracy case. And I'm being tried alone. So you're out of luck."

Richie waved a hand in the air. "I already took care of that. I superceded that indictment so I can have you in this case first." He stood up to go. "You won't get indicted. It will be impossible to link you to what Shorty was up to when you were locked up. But it'll be good to have you around. I want the jury to have you on their mind when it's time to think about whether or not your brother is guilty."

"This is ridiculous."

"Thanks for your assistance."

A few weeks later, I was in the courtroom in Newark, New Jersey standing trial with my brothers. They had a million witnesses they wanted to call to the stand to talk about how awful the "country boys" were and how they destroyed lives with heroin.

One of the people called to the stand was Tommy Nelson's mother. Tommy Nelson was one of our codefendants in the case. His younger brother had died of a drug overdose and his own mother was testifying against us.

When they called her to the stand, I remember Tommy

Nelson whispering, "Momma, please don't do this. Please don't do this."

She went up there anyway.

"Mrs. Nelson, can you tell us how you were impacted by the 'country boys' and their drug operation?"

Mrs. Nelson launched into this long story about her youngest child and how he became addicted to heroin. They must have coached that lady for months on that speech, 'cause I swear if she was onstage she would have won a Tony for her performance. When she talked about seeing her son on the streets, nodding out, I even felt some water coming to my eyes. And I was the one on trial! I looked over at the jury box, and saw some people were openly crying.

"I came home from work one day," Mrs. Nelson said. "And I couldn't find him anywhere. I found him in the bathroom, slumped on the floor, the needle still in his arm. My baby's eyes were wide open. Looked like he'd seen a ghost right before he died. He had those little packets around his body with the words Blue Magic stamped across the top. He was only seventeen years old."

"No further questions, Your Honor," the prosecutor said.

Just about everyone in that damn courtroom was crying, myself included.

I knew we were going down. And sure enough, my brothers were convicted. And I was, too. Even though the jury couldn't really tie me to my brothers, I truly believe that they found me guilty mostly because of Mrs. Nelson's story. They wanted to punish me, too. Since I was sitting right there, why the hell not? There was no way they were going to be able to find me not guilty after that testimony. No way in hell.

Richie came to see me a few weeks later.

"I had no idea they would end up convicting you, too," he said. "I really didn't think that would happen."

"Well, it did. Now what?"

Richie looked really distressed about the whole thing. "I don't know. But I just wanted to come down and tell you in person that I really didn't expect it to go down that way."

Now, I could have said fuck you to Richie. But I didn't. If he was man enough to come down and admit he was wrong to my face, I could be man enough to hear him out.

"Here's what I believe, Frank," he said. "I believe you and your brothers are not the only people who should be punished here. I know about Babyface. I know about the money they took from you when they arrested you. I know there are almost just as many dirty cops out there as there are criminals. And I want to take them down."

I didn't say anything. I just listened. But Richie definitely had my full attention.

"I need proof. I need stories. I need to know which cops are the crooked cops."

"Why should I?"

"You can help redeem yourself."

"That ain't for you to do . . ." I said.

"Okay, never mind redemption. What about a get-out-of-jail-free card?"

I raised my eyebrows and made direct eye contact with Richie. "What are you saying?"

"I'm saying I have a very good relationship with some very important people who are very interested in what you have to say."

"Let me think about it."

"You do that, Frank."

Richie wanted me to rat on cops. Crooked cops. The

ones, like Babyface, who had stolen money from me, the ones who had taken payoffs and bribes from me. Some of them had even take kilos of heroin. I could take them down. I had never been one to drop dime on anyone. It just wasn't how I got down and it had never been necessary. But the cops I'd dealt with were a different story. There was no honor among thieves the way there was among other drug dealers. They would chase me down, curse me out, steal my shit. I thought about them taking down my wife on some stupid obstruction-of-justice charge.

But what really did it for me was one thing: the eleven million dollars that had been in my attic. Those motherfuckers stole it. And no one can tell me different. I know what I brought in my house that night. And there was nothing in the newspaper about it being turned over to the authorities. When Richie came back to see me a few days after he approached me, I knew what I was going to do.

Richie sat across from me, with a pen and a yellow legal notepad.

"We called him Babyface," I began. "Ain't saying his real name. He pulled me over one day, gave me his business card. He was a member of the special investigations unit. He told me he wanted ten thousand a month. I started paying him. He started sending more and more people to me to collect bribes. I ended up paying out millions in protection money. Cash and kilos of heroin, I gave him both from about 1972 until I got locked up. Actually still had to pay him off a few times as I was running things from prison."

Richie scribbled and nodded his head until I stopped speaking. Then he looked up at me.

"Keep going, Frank."

"When am I getting out of here?"

"Soon. With this information? Very soon."

So there you have it. I never snitched on any other dealers, although I know people have said this about me for many years. In a few papers, they would even write things about me testifying against other drug dealers. It's not true. I ratted out crooked cops who were also drug dealers. I ratted out the ones who stole from me after taking an oath to protect and serve. If you think that it's wrong to turn on crooked cops, I don't care. They had never done anything but make my life miserable. If I had to go down, I was taking them down, too.

I ended up becoming friendly with Richie during the weeks that we talked. I helped him figure out which cops were at the top of the chain, the ones he had the best shot at busting. And over so many meetings, we talked about our backgrounds. He was from the streets, had a lot of stories to tell that I could relate to. I think I can say we actually ended up becoming friends.

I've always had this thing. I'm able to talk to anybody about anything. And after a while, they will forget they're talking to a stone-cold criminal. Richie Roberts and I would talk about everything from Motown to boxing and I think I made him feel at ease. Same thing with Sterling Johnson, who was New York's special prosecutor at the time. His job was to bust people like me and put them away for as long as he could. But Sterling Johnson and I were beyond that.

Soon after I gave my information to Richie, they took down the cops just like they said they would. I can't tell you the specifics about who was in charge of springing me out of prison. All I can tell you is this: in the fall of 1981, I was released from prison six years into a forty-year bid. Say what you want about how I got out. The point is, I did. My wife had been released and was living with my daughter in Puerto Rico. I wasn't sure what my next step was going to be. I knew I needed to connect with my wife and reestablish my family. But being out of prison was a weird thing for me. I was starting completely over. I was still Frank Lucas. But I had no shipments coming in from Asia. And it would be a hell of a lot harder to get back over there now that my name and picture had been all over the media.

Now what? Get a job? Hell no. Go back to dealing? Maybe. First, like always, I needed to go somewhere and think.

Billie Mays, who had always stayed in touch with me while I was locked up, picked me up and flew me out to Arizona, where I owned a home that she stayed in occasionally and took care of for me.

"What's your next step going to be?" Billie asked me, as I sat outside by the pool.

"I'm not sure yet," I said, staring at the water.

"Whatever you need, Frank, just let me know. I'll help you any way I can."

"Thanks, Billie."

Billie patted my arm and went back into the house. I had no idea what the next step would be. I knew the feds would be paying very close attention to everything I did. I had the law watching me and it would be difficult to do anything.

But I had no choice but to try. Yes, after being released from prison, I decided I was going right back to the drug game. It was all I knew.

I got in touch with my lieutenant and started making plans to go back to Southeast Asia. My money had dried up, so I needed someone to front me cash to get my operations back in order. It took a few months of conversations and a few plane rides here and there for meetings to get things back up and running. But within a few months of being released, it was looking like I could get back on my feet again.

And then, suddenly, one morning I woke up and realized that although I was getting my business back in order, my personal life was all messed up.

My wife, Julie, was still in Puerto Rico with Francine. I'm ashamed to say that Julie didn't even know I had been released from jail. I just needed a minute to clear my head and think about what the next move would be. But that minute had turned into a few months. And I was dead wrong for that. I needed to be with my family, not Billie. That very morning, I called and booked a flight to New York. After my reservation was finalized, I started packing. Billie came into my bedroom with breakfast on a tray.

"Where are you going?" she asked, placing the tray on the bed.

"Home."

"You are home," she said, her eyes filling with tears.

"No, this is not my home. Home is with my wife and my daughter."

"But, Frank, I thought—"

"I'm sorry if you thought this would be permanent. But you know I'm married. That's where I belong. With my wife and my daughter."

Billie sat down on the bed and burst into tears. "So you're going to just leave?"

It hurt me to see Billie all torn up, but I just had to hope she'd be okay. There was no going back for me. I'd woken up that morning knowing exactly what I needed to do. I couldn't believe I'd stayed out there that long. And that my own wife had no idea I'd even been released. And my little girl was out there, worried sick about me. I called her every week and she was always happy to hear from me. There was no way in the world I could stay in Arizona with Billie.

I can't say I've ever been head-over-heels in love with any woman. And there are a lot of women out there who can say I did them wrong. But right is right. And being with my wife and daughter was the right thing to do.

I never saw Billie again. Someone recently asked me if I wanted to know where Billie is today. I do not want to know. I've never heard one way or another if she's still living. And I don't want to know. If she's alive, I'll feel terrible. She might still be out there thinking about what happened. And if she's dead, I'll feel terrible, knowing she's not here anymore and that I never got a chance to say goodbye. So I don't want to know where she is today.

25

"Daddy, are we gonna stay together, all of us, from now on?"

"Yes, ma'am, we are," I told my daughter Francine.

I was in Las Vegas with Francine and my wife, Julie. We'd all reconnected and were living together as a family again. And I had come out to Vegas to take care of some business. I was dabbling in the game, just enough to keep my head above water. But I wasn't fully in the mix like I wanted to be. I had to take things slow to make sure everything would go on without complications. But of course, Julie was unhappy when I told her my plan.

"After all we've been through," she said, shaking her head. "You want to go back into it."

"What do you think I'm going to do for a living?"

Julie put Francine to bed and then came back out into the living-room area of our suite.

"I don't know, Frank. But we all lost seven years together. I can't believe you would risk not seeing us again. I just can't believe it."

"Can you believe that I need to provide for my family? Can you understand that?"

"So what are you going to do?"

"Whatever I have to do."

As soon as I said that, someone kicked in the door to our hotel room.

"On the floor!" a federal agent screamed.

"Oh my God, Frank," said Julie, "what's happening!"

Julie and I hit the floor as the agents started tearing up the hotel room.

"What the hell is this about?" I said.

"Trying to get back in the game, Frank?"

I had no idea what they were talking about. I was nowhere near where I used to be. At that moment, I had absolutely nothing on me and no one would have been able to tie my name to nothing major. I had no shipments coming in (at least not yet), and nothing really on the horizon that would have warranted all that action.

"I'm not back in anything," I said. "And my daughter is here, right in the next room."

They put another agent in Francine's room while they continued searching our suite. They found nothing but arrested me anyway. Julie was inconsolable. I tried to calm her down but it was no use.

I don't even remember what they tried to charge me with. I just know that the case ended up getting thrown out. I wasn't completely innocent, but I damn sure wasn't as deep in the game as they were trying to make me out to be. But it did let me know that the feds were watching me even closer than I had suspected.

Julie and I got back on our feet. She was taking care of Francine, while I was dabbling in the game, being as careful as I possibly could. But at this point, I really didn't see any options. Even though I knew I was being watched, I still had to do what I had to do. Just like in so many movies and books, I needed one more score. One more opportunity to make a decent payday and then retire. Before, I didn't retire because I wanted a fucking plane. This time, my needs were much simpler. I just needed enough to take care of my family. One or two decent shipments from Southeast Asia and into Harlem would be all I needed. Then I'd use my profits to invest in a few straight businesses. Maybe another nightclub or a restaurant or real estate. Something. Anything.

After a year or so, the heat was off me. My name hadn't been in the papers much and I could tell that I wasn't being watched as closely. And so I made my way back to Southeast Asia and set up another shipment. I kept my operations barebones. I had always had a very close-knit operation. But this time, it was even smaller than usual. I had the least amount of people possible in on the deal and everything went smoothly. Julie didn't even know I was back in the game on that level. And she didn't need to know. I wanted to play everything close to the vest and keep it simple.

I stayed low-profile for two years. I kept my nose clean and made just enough money to survive without bringing too much attention on myself.

At this point, I was over fifty years old. And I was a different person in a lot of ways. I was more mellow, had less of a temper, and I was a lot more laid back and easygoing

than I had been as a younger man. I learned the hard way
that being more laid back was not going to work.

I met a woman I'll call Mariella at a bar in Harlem. Me
and Julie had been going through some changes and we were
off and on. She'd get upset about something and go to Puerto
Rico for a stretch. We'd break up and get back together all
the time. During one of our breaks, I started messing with
this chick Mariella. Nothing serious. I was still married and
planning to stay that way.

The girl was cool even though she came on a bit strong.
She picked me up, not the other way around. She was a pretty
girl so I didn't mind. She was in the game, selling drugs on a
minor level and trying to get on in a major way. She thought
I could help. I told her the truth: my days of rolling like that
were over. I was doing my thing when I needed to. But not in
the way she wanted.

"I don't need you to be in on my deal," she said one night
over dinner. "I just need you to put in a good word for me."

"To who?" I asked.

"This guy from Cuba. I'm trying to get a decent amount
of product from him but he doesn't know me."

"So?"

"He's heard of you. If you just come with me to meet him
and tell him you'll vouch for me, I know he'd put me on."

"I don't work in groups, I told you that. I work alone."

"I know that," she said. "So do I. I told you I'm not asking you to join forces. Just put in a word for me."

I told her no. But she kept needling me about it over a
few weeks and I finally gave in. We went out to a hotel at
LaGuardia and met some guy in the hotel bar.

"You're a legend in this game, Mr. Lucas," he said.

I wasn't feeling him. He was smiling too bright, showing all his teeth. And he seemed to be going out of his way to throw money around. Big tips at the bar, took us to an expensive restaurant. The whole bit. It was just a little over the top. Over dinner, the conversation finally moved from small talk to the real deal.

"Mariella, how much do you want?" the guy asked.

"A half a key," she said.

"And you're sure you can handle it?"

"Absolutely."

The guy looked over at me.

"I stand behind her," I said.

But as soon as I said it, I wanted to take it back. I'd only known the chick for a few weeks. And the whole plan was going down too quick. The day I finally decided to go along with it, she'd set up a meeting for the same exact day. Too fast. But it was done. But in that moment, I decided I wasn't dealing with her anymore. She was using me for my name. I was using her for sex. We were even. And as far as I was concerned, it was over.

I was arrested the very next day for conspiracy to purchase and distribute cocaine.

Mariella was an informant, working for the feds. I'd been set up. The newspaper reports said that I conspired with an undercover agent to set up a drug sale. Which was not true. I hadn't been looking to make a sale with Mariella. She'd approached me. And asked me for help. I pleaded not guilty.

But really, it was all my fault. And it was completely unnecessary. I wasn't even getting any money out of the deal. Just helping out a friend. Or so I thought. I knew from the beginning that there was something off about Mariella and I had not followed my instincts. And that was not like me. While I was on trial and then waiting to be sentenced after being found guilty, I had time to think. And I realized, finally, that this wasn't the right field for me. I wasn't on top of my business like I'd been in the past. I just didn't have the same passion for it all like I used to. I didn't have the same team behind me. I was used to people like Doc Holliday having my back. Now I was doing favors for hot women like Mariella? In the past, I would have never let her into my circle. I was all wrong and on the wrong side of the game. I wasn't a hustler anymore. I was just hustling.

I was sentenced to seven years in federal prison.

This was probably my lowest point. My wife was doing her best without me, raising Francine on her own. I couldn't be there for my family the way I should have been. My son Yogi was in college in Texas, preparing to graduate and join the real world. And his father was getting locked up—again.

I can't say I was starting to regret everything I'd done. To this day, I feel like I did the best with the lot in life I was given. But that jail sentence for trying to help out with Mariella just seemed like a sorry way to end my time in the game. Was that it? Was that going to be my lasting legacy? From a multimillion-dollar industry to going to jail for a half key of coke that wasn't even for me? Straight bullshit.

I'd have a few years to think about it all. And I wasn't looking forward to it.

26

Frank, how are they treating you in here?"

"I can't complain, Martha. How are you?"

"I'm doing well. I heard from Yogi. He's finishing up school."

"I heard. I'm proud of that boy."

"You should be. He's a good kid."

In the visiting room at the federal prison in Phoenix, I sat and talked with one of my frequent visitors, Martha Louis. She was Joe Louis's wife and had always been a very good friend to me and my family. She'd taken Yogi in as one of her own when I was first arrested back in 1975, and she'd taken very good care of him. Martha was an attorney, a very smart, warm, and beautiful woman. And I had a lot of respect for her. By the time I was in prison in Phoenix, Joe Louis had passed away. Martha was still out in Vegas, which meant that she was close enough to Arizona to come to visit. And I appreciated that.

"Yogi is a good kid," I said. "All of my children turned out pretty good. Wish I had been around for them more."

"You did what you knew how to do," Martha said. "You can't beat yourself up now."

"This is the last place I need to be. I'm damn near fifty years old. My family is all over the place. This isn't the way to live."

"So what are you going to do about it?"

"What do you mean?"

"You're getting out soon. What are you going to do?"

"I've gotta figure that out."

I got visits from other friends as well. Candace Louis, Martha's daughter, would come to see me. She was a very sweet girl. And pretty as all outdoors. Opal Brown, who had introduced me to the actress Ena Hartmann, would come out to see me, as well as my old friend Little Pop. It helped the time go by. Three years later, I was sent to a prison camp in Dallas, Texas. Since my son was living there, I opted to go to Dallas so I could be paroled to my son's address and try to get my life together.

"Dad, anything you need, just let me know. I want to help you," Yogi said when I moved into his place in Dallas.

"Son, I want you to concentrate on you. I'll be fine."

"You can stay with me as long as you need to."

"I appreciate that."

"Any idea what you want to do now?"

"Well, I got some ideas about a few business ventures."

"Legal or illegal?"

"Now, Yogi. Don't get all mixed up in what I'm trying to do."

"I was just asking!"

"Well, don't!"

Yogi turned away and left the room. I didn't mean to upset him. But he was asking me questions I didn't have the answers to. How the heck was I supposed to know what to do at my age with no money and no education? All I knew how to do was get back in the game. Something I did not want to do. For a few months, I didn't do much of anything. I caught up with friends and family. I checked in with Julie and Francine, who were living in Puerto Rico. And I flew up to New Jersey to check in on my mother, who had moved north years ago with my father. My father had passed away, but my mother was still kicking, as fiery as ever.

My mom was living in Newark, New Jersey. I stayed with her for a few days before I headed back to Dallas. I had to check in with my parole officer every week so I could never travel for too long. And I hated it. After another trip to my mother's place in Newark, I saw how easy it would be to slip back into hustling, even on a very small level, just to get some money in my pocket.

I found myself in a very bizarre job, a job with a thousand-mile commute. I was living in Dallas with Yogi, checking in with my parole officer every week. And then, two or three times a week or so, I would fly to Newark, stay with my mom, and dabble in the drug game.

I was operating on a very minor level this time. I wasn't even trying to re-create my past glories. There was no point. I wasn't going back to Southeast Asia. I was far from commanding an army of people. Gone were the days of having five hundred people ready to hit the mattresses in my name in the streets of Harlem. There were no shipments coming in. There was no Blue Magic. There was just me, a single entity, making small-time deals with kids who had no idea who I was. I wasn't happy with it. I wanted nothing to do with the game at that point, nothing at all. But I felt like I truly had no other options. It had been all I'd known since I was sixteen years old. What was I supposed to do now? Be a janitor? Work at a fast-food restaurant?

I guess some people would think that spending so much time in jail would have made me give up the game completely. But it didn't. Getting caught and locked up was just an occupational hazard. It never served as a true deterrent. It just came with the territory and I never let the risk stop me. I know I should have. But I never did. I was always thinking about getting out of the game for good. But it never seemed to work out that way.

But traveling back and forth from Newark to Dallas was ridiculous. I wasn't making much money. And here I am, living with my mother and still selling drugs?

One afternoon, I was at my mother's house when I called my parole officer to check in.

"Actually, Frank, I need you to come to my office right now."

"Can't do that," I said. "I can come first thing in the morning."

"Are you in the state of Texas right now, Mr. Lucas?"

"Absolutely," I lied.

"Then you need to get to my office right away. I can't accept a phone check-in today."

"Why not?"

"I need you to get to my office."

"I just told you I am very busy today. I won't be able to get there until the morning."

"Listen here, boy, you need to get to my office immediately."

I hated my parole officer. In fifty years of dealing with the law, I'd come across hundreds of cops, judges, and prosecutors. Some were always fair, even when their job was to put me away. But sometimes, they were just assholes. And this guy was the biggest jerk of all. I could see his face through the phone, pasty white with a fat neck. I hated him.

"You know what?" I said. "Fuck you. Catch me if you can."

I hung up while he was still sputtering into the phone.

And so I was now living with my mother, selling drugs on a small scale, and I was officially on the run. I stayed with my mother and didn't return to Dallas with Yogi. They'd have to find me if they wanted to lock me up for a parole violation. If I'd flown down to Dallas the next day, as I'd planned, he still would have locked me up. I'm sure he knew I wasn't in Texas, where I was supposed to be. So, I was screwed either way. At least, if I didn't go back, I could live life on my own terms—until I got caught.

27

On a fall day in 1991, I ate dinner with my mom as usual and then watched an episode of WWF. My mother was a big fan of wrestling and she didn't miss an episode, especially if Hulk Hogan was scheduled to fight.

"There's no way the Undertaker's gonna beat him," my mother said, settling onto her living-room sofa and turning on the television.

"You think so, huh? We'll see."

"Nobody's beating Hulk Hogan! No one."

"You think I could?"

My mother smiled. "Well, maybe you could, Frank. But nobody else!"

My mother had raised eleven children in abject poverty. I'd seen her work as hard as a man in the fields down in North Carolina. Together, my parents had done the very best they could. I'd provided a decent life for her. When I was doing well in the game, my parents were doing well, too. I'd made sure they had everything they needed. And now, here I was, nearly fifty years old and depending on my mother for food and shelter. I had been taking care of myself since I ran away from the law at age fourteen. I'd never thought things would turn out this way. Never.

In 1975, right before the feds raided my house, I had been just trying to get a private plane. That's all I wanted. A private plane—then I planned to retire. It was supposed to be just that simple. I thought about it all as my mom cheered on Hulk Hogan versus the Undertaker in *WrestleMania VII*. I thought about the look on her face when I showed her the house in Teaneck for the first time.

That night, I went to bed with a heavy heart. Not sure where I would end up next. All I wanted to do was take care of my mother. It would be the least I could do, to make sure she had me for support and companionship.

And of course, that same night, as I lay in bed, I heard a sharp rap on the front door of my mother's house. I turned to look at my nightstand. It was 4:00 A.M. I knew there was only trouble with a visitor at that hour. I went to the door.

"U.S. marshal," a man said, flashing a badge. "You are under arrest for parole violation."

"Come inside," I said.

"No, sir. You need to come with us."

"Well, you're gonna have to wait. I need to tell my mother what's going on."

The marshal actually came inside and took a seat. I'm sure he could tell that I wasn't about to jump out a window or anything like that. I went to my mother's bedroom.

"Mom, wake up," I said, lightly shaking her shoulder.

"Frank, is everything okay?"

"It's okay, Mom. I have to leave, though."

"Right now?"

"Yes, right now."

"Are you in some kind of trouble? What's going on?"

"Don't worry about me, okay, Mom?"

"I'll try, Frank."

I called my sisters Matt and Dora, and told them to keep an eye on our mother. And then I got into the back of the U.S. marshal's car and closed my eyes. It was a short ride from my mother's house in Newark to the Metropolitan Correctional Center in Manhattan. And there I sat, awaiting a hearing on my fate. I had been on lifetime parole, so this violation could have put me in jail for the rest of my life. And I had no one to blame but myself. There was a very good chance that I would die in prison. I had no more lives left. I'd broken the law all my life. And somehow, I'd always managed to squeak by with a lighter sentence than I deserved. I'd had my freedom when I got paroled to Texas. And still, that wasn't enough. I had to go back to the streets once again. And now I was pretty sure it was over for me. I'd never see my children grow up. I'd probably never see the light of day again. Had it been worth it? For the first time, I wasn't sure.

"Mr. Lucas, please come inside and have a seat."

I was led into a conference room at the Metropolitan Correctional Center. I had been in prison for a few weeks, waiting for a meeting with the parole board to determine my fate. I sat down next to my attorney and looked over the people assembled to make the decision. There were five or six elderly white women, dressed in dainty suits and hats, looking like they were on their way to tea with the Queen of England. I couldn't believe it. I'd never had such a saintly, understanding group of women on any jury or parole board before. It almost felt like someone was playing a practical joke on me.

"You are facing lifetime imprisonment for parole violation," said one of the women. "Do you realize the seriousness of the charges you're facing?"

"Yes, I do."

"Mr. Lucas, we have a very difficult task ahead," said one woman, wearing a pale blue pillbox hat. "We have to decide if you are going to be in jail for the rest of your life. Do you think you would be a menace to society if you were released?"

"No, ma'am, I do not."

"What would you do? Where would you live?"

"I would continue living with my mother in New Jersey."

"You're living with your mother right now?"

"Yes, ma'am, I am. And she's getting up there in age and I take care of her."

As we were talking, I saw my sisters being led into the room. They sat down at a nearby table and smiled in my direction. They had bibles in their laps.

"Those are my sisters," I said to the women gathered.

"Would you like to say something about your brother?" one of the women said to my sister Matt.

My sisters spoke on my behalf. They told the women that it was true that I had made some illegal decisions in my life. But they stressed that I was not the same person I had been in my youth. I was older. Maybe wiser in some ways. And most definitely not any threat to society. My sisters must have talked for thirty minutes, urging the parole board to consider letting me go with the lightest penalty possible. After an hour or so of talking, the parole board left the room to discuss my fate and then they all returned.

"What are their options?" I asked my prison counselor.

"They can put you away forever," he said, watching the women as they took their seats. "Or they could put you in jail for a few years and then let you out with lifetime probation."

"What's the bare minimum they could give me?"

"Six months. But don't even think about it. It will never happen."

"Mr. Lucas, we've made a decision."

I sat up straight in my chair and looked them all in the eye, one by one.

"We do believe that you have changed. And we'd like you to be able to continue to care for your mother. We are sentencing you to six months in federal prison."

"I won't be able to take care of my mother from prison," I said.

You would think I was their own child, the way those women looked so sad. The woman speaking looked like she was about to start crying!

"We know, Mr. Lucas. And we considered that. But the law states that the minimum sentence we could give you would be six months."

"I appreciate that," I said. "I really do."

"We're taking a chance on you, Mr. Lucas," said another woman on the parole board. "We hope you understand that you won't have another."

"I understand."

Six months later, I walked out a free man.

I haven't seen the inside of a jail cell since. And I don't plan to. As soon as I got out, my brother Larry asked me about working with him on an oil deal. He knew a man who was trying to import oil from Nigeria to Texas.

"He's got a great connection," said Larry. "He's just trying to raise money."

"Look, Larry," I told my brother. "I'm done with the illegal shit. I ain't going back to prison."

"Nothing illegal here, Frank. He just needs investors. Everything's on the up and up."

"It better be," I said.

I met with the guy and I was impressed with him right away. I agreed to start doing some fund-raising for him and try to get his oil business off the ground. Even though I wasn't in the drug game anymore, I still knew people with money. I ended up raising close to a million dollars in three months. Even my wife, Julie, was able to raise over one hundred thousand dollars through her connections in Puerto Rico.

The profits from the oil business started coming in quickly. It wasn't big money. It was nothing like I'd experienced years before. Nothing at all. But I did pull in about a hundred grand every few months. And I did it legally—for the very first time in my entire adult life.

I could have gotten used to it. But I didn't like that I was working for someone else and not myself. No matter how hard I worked at bringing in investors and making things run smoothly, I was still bringing in the same amount of money. And I wasn't the boss. I didn't know how to not be the boss. That wasn't even in my character. So even though I was making decent money, I quit working in the oil business.

I needed to always do something that was 100 percent mine. Any business I worked in had to be in my name and mine alone.

One of the few things that belonged to me was my story, the wild and crazy tale of my life. And in 2000, I sat down with a writer from *New York Magazine* and told him the truth about who I was and what I'd accomplished in my life. It led me on yet another wild adventure from which I'm still trying to recover.

28

Mr. Lucas, should I drop you off at the red carpet?"

"Drive around the corner one more time."

October: 2007. I'm sitting in the back seat of a limousine with my friends and family. After Marc Jacobson's story on my life appeared in *New York*, Hollywood came calling and optioned the story for film. None other than Denzel Washington was cast to play me. I consulted on the film, met with Denzel a few times to make sure he got it right. And hung out on the set of the film as they shot scenes re-creating my life throughout Harlem.

But on the night of the movie's premiere, I wasn't so sure about facing the flashing lights and reporters' questions. I was all dressed up and ready to go. But something was nagging me. It didn't feel right. We circled the corner once again. There was Jay-Z, who had recorded an album based on the movie.

And Puffy, whose father Melvin I knew so well, Ice-T, and many others. There was Ruby Dee, who played my mother. (My mother passed away before filming began and never got a chance to see our story on film.) Every celebrity you could think of was right there, attached to a project based on my life. It was like nothing I'd ever seen.

"Dad? Are we going inside?"

My son Ray, my youngest, sat next to me, craning his head to get a good look at all the celebrities gathered outside the theater. After I'd been released from jail, I ended up dating a woman who gave birth to my son. He quickly became the light of my life and still is today. I managed to maintain a decent relationship with all of my children; even my oldest, the twins Ruby and Betty, who had been raised in North Carolina. I didn't get to see them as often as I would have liked to. But they were my firstborn children and they would always have a special place in my heart. My boys Yogi and Frankie had always made me proud. And my daughters Francine and Candace were always good girls, sweet and smart kids I'm proud to call my own. And later in life, I had my seventh and youngest child, my son Ray.

Not too long ago, my daughter Francine heard from a young man named Rodney. His mother, a woman I used to date named Pauline, told him that I was his daddy and he said he'd been looking for me ever since. Now, when the movie started filming, you would have thought I had twenty children, the way people were trying to reach me telling me I was their daddy. But Rodney is different. Looks like he could be mine. I'm not sure. But if he is, that's my eighth child right there.

And Julie? Oh, we've been off and on for years. More on than off. A few years ago, she came over to my place to visit when she was up here from Puerto Rico. She's been here with me ever since. Truth is, no matter what's happened or how many times we've gone back and forth, she's still my wife. Always will be.

At any rate, by the night of the movie premiere, I was living close to my family and helping them all out in any way I could. And I was thoroughly done with the street life. I made a little money from consulting on the film and was able to live comfortably.

So why couldn't I go down the red carpet? Why couldn't I enjoy the feeling of knowing that my story might have been able to prevent some people from making all the same mistakes I made?

"Dad? What do you want to do?" my son Ray said. "Julie's going inside. And so is Francine."

"Don't you want to go in, Frank?" said one of my nephews, as the driver circled the block once again.

"I don't know. . . ."

"This is big, Dad!" said Ray.

"Yeah," I said. "I guess so."

But the truth was, it wasn't exciting for me. I was no stranger to glitz and glamour. I'd owned nightclubs. I'd counted all kinds of celebrities as my friends. Seeing a bunch of celebrities gathered wasn't a big deal to me. The only difference was that they were gathered to watch a film about me. Something based on my life and my actions. It felt strange. It wasn't like I was being honored. But in some ways, that's what I felt like. People wanted to see me, shake my hand, talk to me, hear my story.

I could understand why. I had experienced enough for ten movie scripts.

But I had done some things I wasn't proud of. The day that

woman testified in court about what drugs did to her son, it hit home for me and I realized what kind of damage I had been responsible for. I didn't stop hustling after that day, but I never forgot it. And it really had an impact on how I looked at the whole game. And then, when those elderly women on the parole board gave me another chance at freedom, I really took it as a sign that I had to go the right way.

I didn't feel like glad-handing a crowd of people who thought I was in any way cool because of my past or because Denzel Washington was now playing me in a big-budget film.

"We can go home," I said to the driver.

"Are you sure, sir?"

I looked at the crowd gathered one more time in front of the Apollo Theater.

"Yes," I said. "I'm sure."

In some small measure, my absence from the premiere was out of respect to the many people, in Harlem and beyond, who suffered from the heroin industry that I helped to expand. Over the thirty years that I was in the game, millions of people succumbed to heroin addiction. Families were torn apart. Husbands, fathers, mothers, and wives overdosed. There were some people who had managed to recover and redeem themselves from a lifetime of addiction.

I was still hoping to redeem myself. I'd had a major role in making the drugs available and profiting from that negativity.

I stayed away from the glitz and glamour that night. Out of respect. Today, I write this book and outline all my successes and my failings in honor of every single person affected directly or indirectly by the evils of the heroin trade. I made some decisions that affected many people in my life. I'm seventy-eight years old today and I still have a lifetime of regret.

And every word in this book is dedicated to those I impacted in any way.

INDEX